Twist & Sprout® Cookbook

240 menus for childcare providers

developed by Providers Choice

Twist & Sprout Cookbook—240 Menus for Childcare Providers
Providers Choice, Inc.
© 2016 Providers Choice, Inc.

First edition

Providers Choice Press
10901 Red Circle Drive, Suite 100
Minnetonka, MN 55343

To order, visit ProvidersChoice.com or call 800-356-5983

ISBN: 9780692809341_0-00

Printed in the United States of America

Table of Contents

Introduction

We hope you love this cookbook as much as we do! Developed and written in the Twist & Sprout® kitchen at Providers Choice, the *Twist & Sprout Cookbook* is for all of you who "Love for a Living."

Children develop rapidly during the first five years of life and—with the right nutrition—will develop and grow to their full physical and mental potential. By providing the children with more than half of their meals and snacks each day you are delivering very important key nutrients to each child. You are also teaching them to embrace new experiences and new foods while creating healthy eating habits which they will carry with them for the rest of their lives.

The Child and Adult Care Food Program (CACFP) recognizes the critical role that food plays in children's lives and the CACFP meal guidelines ensure that your children are receiving the nutrients they require to grow and thrive. Studies repeatedly show that children in CACFP facilities receive meals that are nutritionally superior to those served by facilities that are not part of this program. This is important to parents and should be a key part of your marketing message.

This cookbook is designed to make your job easier by providing you with a four-week cycle menu for each season—spring, summer, autumn and winter. Each day includes menus for breakfast, lunch and snack with proper crediting for the CACFP. All meals and menus meet the new USDA Meal Pattern requirements, effective October 1st, 2017. Equally important, all the recipes are chef-developed and kid-tested.

Your kids will love the recipes! We suggest you share them with your kids' parents to help their families eat healthier at home. This also demonstrates to parents some of the important things you are doing for their children.

About Providers Choice

Founded in 1985, Providers Choice, Inc. (PCI) has grown to become the largest Child and Adult Care Food Program (CACFP) sponsor in the state of Minnesota and in the nation, serving both family child care providers and child care centers. PCI's mission is to administer the USDA Child and Adult Care Food Program for child care facilities and provide education, enrichment and assistance to persons providing child care services. This is done to insure the health and well-being of children in child care, to stretch and support caregivers and to promote child care as a profession.

Providers Choice has a strong national presence which enables us to have a voice in Washington. Our company has been represented on the board of directors of the National CACFP Sponsors Association; was invited to the White House by President Bill Clinton to participate in the first White House Conference on Child Care; asked to serve on the USDA 5-Star Child Nutrition Task Force to develop the CACFP logo and tagline *Where Healthy Eating Becomes a Habit*; and asked to participate on the USDA Paperwork Reduction Task Force in Washington, D.C. Providers Choice has also been very active and involved with providing input to the USDA on the New Meal Pattern requirements.

As a leader in the field, PCI has led the charge against childhood obesity with innovative training in nutrition, most recently implementing Health and Wellness in the Day Care Setting and the Twist and Sprout: Cultivating Healthier Child Care Initiative. These innovative programs were a result of partnering with other organizations such Center for Prevention at Blue Cross Blue Shield of Minnesota, Hunger Impact Partners and the Cargill Foundation.

Providers Choice looks forward to serving many more years as a voice for children, families and child care providers.

Acknowledgements

A Special Thank You

A work of this magnitude cannot happen without the contributions of many individuals. The dedication and passion of the following people enabled us to produce a great cookbook for anyone cooking for kids.

The Chef Marshall O'Brien Group has been an integral part of our Twist & Sprout initiative since its beginning in November 2013. The menus and recipes in this book were developed by Chef Marshall. His time and talents are always appreciated.

Providers Choice nutritionist, Kate Abernathy, MS, RDN, and Joanne Norman spent many hours reviewing and updating the menus and recipes to ensure they meet the new USDA meal pattern requirements that take effect October 1, 2017.

Many of us who use cookbooks admit that most of the recipes we prepare are the ones that have a picture of the item. A big thank you goes to Amy Zellmer of Custom Creations Photography, whose talents brought these dishes to life.

Of course, you can't take photographs without something to photograph. Our amazing Providers Choice staff prepared and styled all of the recipes in this book. We have tasted every recipe and have many favorites as a result.

After all the pieces are completed, a project must be pulled together. We could not have chosen a more skilled and talented designer and project manager than Bonnie McDermid of Wordsmith Ink. Bonnie went above and beyond to bring us a product that we are proud to share with you.

We appreciate the funding from Center for Prevention at Blue Cross and Blue Shield of Minnesota for the Twist & Sprout Initiative. Our cookbook was made possible through the generous support of the Cargill Foundation.

How to Use this Book

We created the Twist and Sprout cookbook with you in mind. All recipes and menus are in compliance with required Child and Adult Care Food Program regulations and include many CACFP best practices. Fruits and vegetables were chosen for each season based on seasonality and affordability. Many recipes were designed to save you time in the kitchen while focusing on health and wellness.

This cookbook provides 240 menu ideas that meet the updated Child and Adult Care Food Program (CACFP) Meal Patterns, effective October 1, 2017. Menus are arranged into seasons with a four-week cycle menu for each season.

Each day includes a menu for breakfast, lunch and one snack complete with colorful photos, recipes and crediting information. The grid below each photo shows the minimum portion size required for each age group. Icons next to each recipe indicate which meal components are included in that recipe.

Icon Key

 Bread = Grains component
Abbreviated as GB for Grain/Bread

 Meat = Meat or Meat Alternate component
Abbreviated as MMA for Meat/Meat Alternate

 Carrot = Vegetable component
Abbreviated as VEG for Vegetable

 Apple = Fruit component
Abbreviated as FR for Fruit

Sample Portion Grid

Indicates the minimum portion sizes required for a creditable/reimbursable meal with the CACFP. An asterisk (*) indicates menu items that have a recipe.

	Toddler	Pre-School	School Age
Chicken*	1/3 cup	1/2 cup	2/3 cup
Couscous	1/4 cup	1/4 cup	1/2 cup
Carrots*	1/8 cup	1/4 cup	1/2 cup
Salad	1/4 cup	1/2 cup	1/2 cup
Milk	1/2 cup	3/4 cup	1 cup

Every effort was made to ensure proper crediting of all menus and recipes. Providers Choice, Inc. cannot guarantee the crediting information in this book for non-Providers Choice providers; we recommend checking with your individual sponsoring organization.

Spring Menus
Weeks One & Two

Spring	Monday	Tuesday	Wednesday	Thursday	Friday
Week One					
Breakfast	Oatmeal Squares* Peaches Yogurt Milk	Get Up & Go French Toast* Strawberry Bursts Milk	Sweet Corn Quesadilla* Apples Milk	Southwest Breakfast Wrap* Strawberries Milk	Blueberry Pancakes* Hard Boiled Egg Blueberries Milk
Lunch	Pasta with Turkey Tomato Sauce* Sugar Snap Peas Grapes Milk	Melty Tomato-Cheese Sandwich* Peas Banana Milk	Quick Moroccan Chicken* Whole Grain Couscous Honey-Glazed Carrots* Spinach Salad Milk	Ham and Cheese Roll-Ups* Celery Cucumber Slices Milk	Mediterranean Quinoa* Broccoli Cantaloupe Milk
Snack	Garden Basil Triangles*	Butternut Squash Cornbread Muffin* Blueberries	Peaches Milk	Spiced Chickpeas* Milk	Creamy Fruit Dip* Apples
Week Two					
Breakfast	Hammy Scrambled Eggs* Whole Grain Toast Grapes Milk	Apple Z Muffins* Orange Wedges Milk	Pretty Parfait* Milk	Breakfast Sandwich* Apple Fans Milk	Sweetheart Pancakes with Strawberry Compote* Milk

Lunch	Toasty Cheesy
	  Bean Sandwiches*
	Sauteed Parsnips*
	Mandarin Oranges
	Milk
		Creamy Carrot Soup*
		Whole Grain Crackers
		Cheese
		Blueberries
		Milk
			Tasty Tacos*
			Corn
			Grapes
			Milk
				Teriyaki Turkey Burger
				  on Whole Grain Bun*
				Baked Beans
				Peaches
				Milk
					Chicken Stir-Fry *
					Savory Brown Rice*
					Celery
					Peppy Pineapple
					Milk

Snack	Apple Wedges String Cheese	Banana-Strawberry Hats* Milk	Black Bean Dip* Red Pepper Strips	Parmesan Zucchini Crisps* Milk	String Cheese Broccoli Trees

Spring Menus
Weeks Three & Four

Week Three					
Spring	**Monday**	**Tuesday**	**Wednesday**	**Thursday**	**Friday**
Breakfast	Green Egg Popper* Whole Grain Toast Peaches Milk	Breakfast Frushi* Milk	Berry Nice Oatmeal* Milk	Good Morning Sunshine* Milk	Blueberry Crepes* Milk
Lunch	Black Bean Taco Salad* Whole Grain Corn Chips Grapes Milk	Cheesy Chicken Pizza* Green Beans Apple Slices Milk	Broccoli-Beef Bowl* Brown Rice Mandarin Oranges Milk	Crazy Quinoa* Corn Strawberries Milk	Spicy Shredded Beef* on Whole Grain Bun Peas Cantaloupe Milk
Snack	Creamy Zucchini Crackers*	Strawberry-Kiwi Salsa* Whole Grain Tortilla Crisps*	Yummy Yams* Milk	Edamame Dip* Vegetable Sticks Toast Triangles	Cinnamon Apples* Cottage Cheese
Week Four					
Breakfast	PBJ Roll-Up* Cantaloupe Bites Milk	Banana Bread* Banana Wheels Milk	Sweet Quinoa* Scrambled Eggs Strawberries Milk	Slow Cooker Oatmeal* Milk	Super Strata* Blueberries Milk
Lunch	Inside-Out Roast Beef Sandwich* Summertime Carrots* Peppy Pineapple Milk	Chicken Pizza Puffs* Spinach Salad Grapes Milk	Taco-Style Lentils & Rice* Peas Mandarin Oranges Milk	Broccoli-Cheese Bites* Whole Grain Crackers Sugar Snap Peas Cantaloupe Milk	Mighty Spinach-Chicken Quesadilla* Jicama Sticks Honeydew Drops Milk
Snack	Strawberries Milk	Zucchini Chips* Whole Grain Crackers	Carrot Fries* Milk	Grapes Whole Grain Crackers	Peanutty Yogurt Dip* Apple Fans

Summer Menus
Weeks One & Two

Summer	Monday	Tuesday	Wednesday	Thursday	Friday
Week One					
Breakfast	Happy Flapjacks* Hard Boiled Egg Strawberries Milk	Sugar and Spice Quesadilla* Milk	Parfait Smoothie* Milk	Baked Omelet* Whole Grain Toast Mil	Breakfast Banana Splits* Milk
Lunch	Sloppy Sammie* on Whole Grain Bun Peas Watermelon Milk	Green Garden Salad* Breadsticks Apples Milk	Black Bean, Corn and Blueberry Salad* Whole Grain Bread Grilled Asparagus Milk	BBQ Chicken Wraps* Cucumber Slices Peppy Pineapple Milk	Island Fun Pasta Salad* Cherry Tomatoes Celery Sticks Milk
Snack	Funky Cabbage Salad* Milk	Watermelon Pizza*	Sweet Potato Crisps* Milk	Frozen Strawberries and Yogurt*	Three Shape Trail Mix* Grapes
Week Two					
Breakfast	Sunny Fiesta Wrap* Grapes Milk	Almond-Raisin Granola* Peaches Milk	Oh My Oatmeal* Milk	Whole Grain Bagel Nut Butter Honeydew Drops Milk	Scrambled Eggs Whole Grain Toast Blueberries Milk
Lunch	Q Burgers* Shredded Lettuce Salad Apples Milk	Chinese Pork* Whole Grain Roll Cabbage Steaks* Carrots Sticks Grapes Milk	Baked Meatballs* Blooming Bulgur* Peas Pineapple Milk	Summertime Rice* Roasted Broccoli Trees Pears Milk	Fun Fish Nuggets* Citrus Couscous* Corn and Peas Orange Wedges Milk
Snack	Sweet Strawberry Pudding*	Monkey Milk Shake* Whole Grain Crackers	Herb Bagel Crisps* Applesauce	Cool as a Cucumber Dip* Carrot Sticks	Bold Black Bean Dip* Sugar Snap Peas

Summer Menus
Weeks Three & Four

Week Three					
Summer	**Monday**	**Tuesday**	**Wednesday**	**Thursday**	**Friday**
Breakfast	Crunchy Fruit Kabobs* Milk	Pancake Smiles* Berries Milk	Fruity Quinoa* Milk	Eggs in a Nest Apple Bites Milk	Cinnamon Berry Treasures* Milk
Lunch	Golden Spiced Chicken* Whole Grain Roll Spinach and Radish Wheel Salad Watermelon Bites Milk	Turkey Apple Takers* Broccoli Trees Citrus Corn* Milk	Sweet Swirl Wrap* Celery Sticks Grapes Milk	Roast Pork with Red Pepper Sauce* Savory Brown Rice Mighty Minty Peas* Banana Wheels Milk	Captain's Zesty Chicken* Power Penne* Peach Smiles Milk
Snack	Gooey Towers*	Peachy Smoothie*	Cucumber Canoes* Milk	Go Fish Snack* Carrot Sticks	Pineapple-Cottage Cheese Yummies*
Week Four					
Breakfast	Bananas Foster Parfait* Milk	Little Boy Blue Muffins* Blueberries Milk	Rise and Shine Cereal* Milk	Farmers Pizza* Grapes Milk	Toasted O's Cereal Strawberries Milk
Lunch	Italian Flag Pasta* Awesome Asparagus* Grapes Milk	Summertime Tuna Bites* Broccoli Slaw Peas Milk	Picnic Pinwheels* Cucumber Spears Watermelon Milk	Colorful Roll-Up* Whole Grain Roll Cantaloupe Moons Milk	Pocket of Gold* Roasted Parmesan Potatoes* Peaches Milk
Snack	Green Pepper Posies* Milk	Crunchy Rosemary Chickpeas* Milk	Mr. Tomato Head*	Sunflower Snacks*	Ants on a Raft* Milk

Autumn Menus
Weeks One & Two

Autumn	Monday	Tuesday	Wednesday	Thursday	Friday
Week One					
Breakfast	Fiesta Egg Puff* Whole Grain Toast Milk	Banana Rama Breakfast* Milk	Apple Snapple Oatmeal* Milk	Oatmeal-Carrot Muffin* Banana Milk	Hocus Pocus Pancakes* Scrambled Eggs Applesauce Milk

Lunch	Beany Power Pita*
	Carrot & Celery Sticks
	Applesauce
	Milk
		Olé Chicken Tostada*
		Roasted Broccoli &
		  Cauliflower Crowns*
		Pear Rings
		Milk
			English Muffin
			  Vegetable Pizza*
			Lovely Little Peas
			Peaches
			Milk
				Scrumptious Chicken
				  Drumsticks*
				Whole Grain Roll
				Green Beans
				Pineapple
				Milk
					Lavish Lasagna*
					Spinach Salad
					Orange Smiles
					Milk

Snack	Cauliflower Popcorn* Milk	Whole Grain Crackers Apple Slices	Hummus Dip* Carrots	Cinnamon Toast Warm-You-Up Cider*	Peaches Yogurt
Week Two					
Breakfast	Veggie Pancakes* Orange Smiles Milk	Super Fruity Salsa* Whole Grain Toast Milk	Scrambled Eggs Whole Grain Toast Banana Milk	Hungry Bunny Muffin* String Cheese Grapes Milk	Gorgeous Granola* Blueberries Milk
Lunch	Oven Sloppy Joes* on Whole Grain Bun Spunky Spinach* Crazy Crinkle Carrots Milk	Little Bo Peep Pot Pie* Jicama Sticks Watermelon Milk	Long Live Lemon Chicken* Whole Grain Roll Tiny Tasty Edamame Mandarin Oranges Milk	Rainbow Turkey Wrap* Cheery Cherry Tomatoes Cucumber Slices Apple Rings Milk	Sweet Salmon* Brown Rice Sugar Snap Peas Red Pepper Slices Milk
Snack	Apple Boats Milk	Roasted Chickpeas* Milk	Big League Black Bean Salsa* Whole Grain Tortilla Chips	Pumpkin Pie Dip* Mini-Pretzels	Clementine Pumpkins* Yogurt Raspberries

9

Autumn Menus
Weeks Three & Four

Week Three					
Autumn	Monday	Tuesday	Wednesday	Thursday	Friday
Breakfast	Peachy Parfait* Milk	Whole Grain Toast Blueberries Milk	Poofy Puffy Pancake* Plums Milk	Whole Grain Cereal Scrambled Eggs Banana Milk	Awesome Oatmeal* Fruit Topping* Milk

Lunch	Tropical Turkey Meatloaf*
	Whole Grain Roll
	Green Beans
	Clever Cauliflower
	Milk
		Super Italian Pasta*
		Banana
		Milk
			Pumped Up Red Peppers*
			Zippy Cucumbers
			Peaches
			Milk
				Marvelous Hummus
				  Sandwich*
				Carrot Sticks
				Honeydew Melon
				Milk
					Mighty Meatballs with
					  Rock'n Ragu Sauce*
					Whole Wheat Roll
					Broccoli Crowns
					Mixed Fruit
					Milk

Snack	Apples Yogurt	Grand Pear Gondolas* Milk	Sassy Sweet Potato Fries* Milk	Curry Yogurt Dip* Celery Sticks	Cheese Stick Apple Slices
Week Four					
Breakfast	Green Machine Smoothie* Whole Grain Toast Milk	Viva La Veggie Scrambler* Whole Grain Tortilla Milk	Perky Pancakes* Orange Smiles Milk	Sunshine Muffin* Grapes Milk	Breakfast Burrito Swirls* Apple Fans Milk
Lunch	Buddy Bows & Veggies* Spinach Salad Fruit Kabobs Milk	Hearty Pot Roast* Whole Grain Roll Cantaloupe Milk	Pretzel Chicken* Whole Grain Bread Bionic Brussels Sprouts* Peaches Milk	Tasty Turkey Tomato Bites* Brown Rice Pilaf* Tiny Tasty Edamame Milk	Silly Dilly Chicken Soup* Whole Grain Crackers Pineapple Milk
Snack	Goofy Grapes Whole Grain Crackers	Monkey Ice* Milk	Pretzel Rods Sliced Plums	Blast Off Black Bean Dip* Carrot Sticks	Mini Trees String Cheese

Winter Menus
Weeks One & Two

Week One					
Winter	Monday	Tuesday	Wednesday	Thursday	Friday
Breakfast	Crazy Corn Cakes* Fruit Milk	Super Power Oatmeal* Hard Boiled Egg Blueberries Milk	Whole Grain English Muffin Nutty Nut Butter Orange Smiles Milk	Whole Grain Toast Banana Milk	Eggerific Muffin Sandwich* Apple Wedges Milk
Lunch	Pizazz Pocket Pizza* Green Pepper Squares Banana Milk	Aloha Tuna Melt* Chimney Chili Carrots* Milk	Cheesy Butternut Mac* Broccoli Trees Pears Milk	Chill 'n Chili* Whole Grain Crackers Honeydew Drops Milk	Lotta Veggie Turkey Sammie* Groovy Green Beans Peaches Milk
Snack	Grapes Whole Grain Crackers	Apple Wedges Milk	Stuffed Celery* Milk	Peaches Yogurt	Winter King's Cottage Cheese* Carrot Spears
Week Two					
Breakfast	Superstar Breakfast* Milk	Creamy Apple Wrap* Milk	Big Dipper Parfait* Milk	Morning Fun Muffin* String Cheese Peaches Milk	Scrambled Eggs Whole Grain Cereal Banana Milk
Lunch	Cheesy Chicken Quesadilla* Cauliflower Clouds Mandarin Bursts Milk	Sassy Salmon* Awesome Asian Rice* Lovely Little Peas Peppy Pineapple Milk	Fun Frijole Wrap* Broccoli Trees Apple Cubes Milk	Chicken Tango Triangles* Spinach Salad Orange Wedges Milk	Mighty Meatloaf* Whole Grain Roll Amazing Acorn Squash* Cantaloupe Bites Milk
Snack	Apple Boats Milk	Hummus* Bell Pepper Strips	All-Star Snack* Milk	Cheese Crispies* Milk	Bunny Juice* Whole Grain Crackers

Winter Menus
Weeks Three & Four

Week Three					
Winter	**Monday**	**Tuesday**	**Wednesday**	**Thursday**	**Friday**
Breakfast	Fruity Toast* Milk	Berry Blueberry Muffin* Blueberries Milk	Broccoli Mini Bake* Whole Grain Toast Clementines Milk	Apple Pancakes* Hard Boiled Egg Milk	Whole Grain Bagel Nut Butter Curried Peachy Pears* Milk
Lunch	Beany Pizza Patties* Whole Grain Bun Spinach Salad Apple Slices Milk	Chicken Bites* Whole Wheat Roll Tangy Sweet Potatoes* Groovy Grapes Milk	Potato Vegetable Chowder* Cracker Stackers* Banana Milk	Lovable Lentils* Whole Grain Roll Broccoli Crowns Pineapple Triangles Milk	Teriyaki Chicken* Savory Brown Rice* Carrot Sticks Green Pepper Strips Milk
Snack	Turkey Roll-Ups*	Tomato Bruschetta*	Baking Powder Biscuits* Pear Boats	Tomato Treats*	Cranberry-Apple Salad* Milk
Week Four					
Breakfast	Sunshine Scrambler* Whole Grain Toast Mandarin Oranges Milk	Mexican Migas* Banana Milk	Goldilocks Porridge* Blueberries Milk	Cranberry-Sweet Potato Muffin* Pineapple Triangles Milk	Zesty Breakfast Wrap* Milk
Lunch	Tasty Tomato-Basil Pasta* Cucumber Wheels Banana Milk	Wonderful Winter Soup* Whole Wheat Roll Peaches Milk	Pizza Wheels Broccoli Trees Apple Wedges Milk	Chicken Caesar Wraps Carrot Spears Great Grapes Milk	Oven Beef Stew* Whole Grain Crackers Orange Smiles Milk
Snack	Apple-Rice Delight*	Blizzard Fruit Mix* Milk	Crispy Carrot Coleslaw* Milk	Rosy Mozzarella Bites* Milk	Spinach Boats

Child Meal Patterns

Breakfast

	Ages 1-2	Ages 3-5	Ages 6-11
Milk, fluid, low-fat or fat-free	1/2 cup	3/4 cup	1 cup
Fruit or Vegetable	1/4 cup	1/2 cup	1/2 cup
Grain or Meat/Meat Alternate			
Bread; whole grain-rich or enriched bread	1/2 slice	1/2 slice	1 slice
Cereal; cold, dry or hot, cooked	1/4 cup	1/3 cup	3/4 cup
Lean meat, poultry or fish	1/2 oz.	1/2 oz.	1 oz.
Large egg	1/2	1/2	1/2
Yogurt	1/4 cup (2 oz.)	1/4 cup (2 oz.)	1/2 cup (4 oz.)

Snack
(select 2 of 5 components)

	Ages 1-2	Ages 3-5	Ages 6-11
Milk, fluid, low-fat or fat-free	1/2 cup	1/2 cup	1 cup
Meat/Meat Alternate	1/2 oz.	1/2 oz.	1 oz.
Nut Butter	1 tbsp.	1 tbsp.	1 tbsp.
Yogurt	1/4 cup (2 oz.)	1/4 cup (2 oz.)	1/2 cup (4 oz.)
Fruit	1/2 cup	1/2 cup	3/4 cup
Vegetable	1/2 cup	1/2 cup	3/4 cup
Grain or Meat/Meat Alternate			
Bread; whole grain-rich or enriched bread	1/2 slice	1/2 slice	1 slice
Cereal; cold, dry	1/4 cup	1/3 cup	3/4 cup

Lunch

	Ages 1-2	Ages 3-5	Ages 6-11
Milk, fluid, low-fat or fat-free	1/2 cup	3/4 cup	1 cup
Meat/Meat Alternate			
Lean meat, poultry, fish, tofu	1 oz.	1-1/2 oz.	2 oz.
Cheese	1 oz.	1-1/2 oz.	2 oz.
Large egg	1/2	3/4	1
Cooked dry beans/peas	1/4 cup	3/8 cup	1/2 cup
Nut or seed butters	2 tbsp.	3 tbsp.	4 tbsp.
Yogurt	1/2 cup (4 oz.)	3/4 cup (6 oz.)	1 cup (8 oz.)
Nuts and/or seeds	1/2 oz. = 50%	3/4 oz. = 50%	1 oz. = 50%
Vegetable	1/8 cup	1/4 cup	1/2 cup
Fruit or second vegetable	1/8 cup	1/4 cup	1/4 cup
Vegetable	1/2 cup	1/2 cup	3/4 cup
Grain			
Bread; whole grain-rich or enriched bread	1/2 slice	1/2 slice	1 slice
Pasta or rice	1/4 cup	1/4 cup	1/2 cup

Notes to Child Meal Patterns:
1. Unflavored whole milk for children age one, unflavored low-fat (1%) or fat-free (skim) milk for children over age two.
2. Juice is limited to one time per day.
3. At least one serving per day must be whole grain-rich.
4. Meat/meat alternates may replace the grain component a maximum of three times per week.
5. Breakfast cereals may contain no more than 6 grams of total sugar per dry ounce.
6. Yogurt may contain no more than 23 grams of total sugar per 6 ounces.

Infant Meal Patterns

Breakfast, Lunch or Supper	
Birth-5 months	6-11 months
4-6 fluid oz. breastmilk or iron-fortified infant formula	6-8 fluid oz. breastmilk or iron-fortified infant formula **AND** 0-4 tbsp. iron-fortified infant cereal, meat, fish, poultry, whole egg, beans; **OR** 0-2 oz. cheese or 0-4 oz. cottage cheese; **OR** 0-8 oz. (1 cup) yogurt or a combination of the above **AND** 0-2 tbsp. vegetable or fruit or a combination of both*

Snack	
Birth-5 months	6-11 months
4-6 fluid oz. breastmilk or iron-fortified infant formula	2-4 fluid oz. breastmilk or iron-fortified infant formula **AND** 0-1/2 slice of bread; or 0-2 crackers; or 0-4 tbsp. iron-fortified infant cereal or ready-to-eat breakfast cereal; **AND** 0-2 tbsp. vegetable or fruit or a combination of both*

*Fruit and vegetable juices are not reimbursable on the infant meal pattern.

CACFP Optional Best Practices

USDA highly encourages the implementation of these optional best practices in order to ensure children are getting the optimal benefit from meals they receive while in care:

Infants

- Support mothers who choose to breastfeed their infants by encouraging mothers to supply breastmilk and offer a quiet, private area that is comfortable and sanitary for mothers who come to breastfeed.

Vegetables & Fruits

- Serve a vegetable or fruit with snack daily.
- Serve a variety of fruits and choose whole fruits (fresh, canned, dried, or frozen) more often than juice.
- Provide at least one serving each of dark green vegetables, red and orange vegetables, beans and peas (legumes), starchy vegetables, and other vegetables once per week.

Grains

- Serve whole grain-rich grains twice per day.

Meat & Meat Alternate

- Serve only lean meats, nuts, and legumes.
- Serve processed meats less than once per week.
- Serve only natural cheeses and choose low-fat or reduced fat-cheeses.

Additional Best Practices

- Incorporate local, seasonal produce into meals.
- Limit serving purchased pre-fried foods to no more than one serving per week.
- Avoid serving non-creditable foods that are sources of added sugars, such as sweet toppings, mix-in ingredients sold with yogurt and sugar-sweetened beverages (e.g., fruit drinks or sodas).

Spring Recipes

twist & sprout

SPRING Week 1 Monday

Breakfast

Oatmeal Squares, Peaches, Yogurt, Milk

	Toddler	Pre-School	School Age
Oatmeal Squares*	1 square	1 square	2 squares
Peaches	1/4 cup	1/2 cup	1/2 cup
Yogurt	1/4 cup	1/4 cup	1/2 cup
Milk	1/2 cup	3/4 cup	1 cup

Lunch

Pasta with Turkey Tomato Sauce, Sugar Snap Peas, Grapes, Milk

	Toddler	Pre-School	School Age
Pasta*	1/4 cup	1/4 cup	1/2 cup
Tomato Sauce*	1/2 cup	2/3 cup	3/4 cup
Snap Peas	1/8 cup	1/4 cup	1/2 cup
Grapes	1/8 cup	1/4 cup	1/4 cup
Milk	1/2 cup	3/4 cup	1 cup

Snack

Garden Basil Triangles

	Toddler	Pre-School	School Age
Garden Basil Triangles*	2 triangles	2 triangles	4 triangles

Breakfast

Oatmeal Squares

1½ cups quick oats
½ cup whole wheat flour
½ teaspoon baking soda
½ teaspoon salt
1 teaspoon ground cinnamon
1 egg
1 cup 1% or fat-free milk
3 tablespoons applesauce
¼ cup brown sugar

1. Preheat oven to 350 degrees. Coat an 8 x 8-inch baking pan with cooking spray.

2. In large bowl, mix all ingredients together until just combined. Pour batter into prepared pan.

3. Bake for 20 minutes or until a toothpick inserted into the center comes out clean.

4. Allow to cool for 5 minutes and cut into 16 squares.

Makes 16 squares

  1 square provides 0.5 oz. GB
  for a 3-5 year old at breakfast

Lunch

Pasta with Turkey Tomato Sauce

1 cup uncooked whole grain pasta
1 tablespoon olive oil
⅓ cup onions, chopped small
1 pound ground turkey
1 teaspoon Italian seasoning
1½ cups low-sodium marinara sauce

1. Prepare pasta according to package directions.

2. In skillet or small saucepan over medium heat, add oil, onions and turkey.

3. Cook and brown turkey until almost cooked through, about 5 minutes. Add Italian seasoning. Mix well.

4. Add marinara sauce and mix well. Heat until sauce is hot. Serve over pasta.

Makes about 4 cups

  ¼ cup pasta and ⅔ cup sauce provide
  0.5 oz. GB and 1.5 oz. MMA for a 3-5 year
  old at lunch/supper

Snack

Garden Basil Triangles

3 large whole wheat pita rounds,
  each cut into 4 triangles
3 ounces mozzarella cheese,
  cut into bite-sized squares
1½ cups fresh tomatoes, sliced
⅓ cup fresh basil, julienned

1. Arrange triangles on sheet pan. Brush a little olive oil on each triangle.

2. Toast slightly underneath broiler. Remove from heat.

3. Top each pita triangle with the cheese, tomato slices and basil.

Makes 12 pita triangles

  2 triangles provide 0.5 oz. GB and 0.5 oz.
  MMA for a 3-5 year old at snack

SPRING Week 1 Tuesday

Breakfast

Get Up & Go French Toast, Strawberry Bursts, Milk

	Toddler	Pre-School	School Age
French Toast*	1/2 slice	1/2 slice	2 half slices
Strawberry Bursts	1/4 cup	1/2 cup	1/2 cup
Milk	1/2 cup	3/4 cup	1 cup

Lunch

Melty Tomato Cheese Sandwich, Peas, Bananas, Milk

	Toddler	Pre-School	School Age
Sandwich*	2 sandwiches	2 sandwiches	3 sandwiches
Peas	1/4 cup	1/2 cup	1/2 cup
Banana	1/4	1/2	1/2
Milk	1/2 cup	3/4 cup	1 cup

Snack

Butternut Squash Cornbread Muffins, Blueberries

	Toddler	Pre-School	School Age
Cornbread*	1/2 muffin	1/2 muffin	1 muffin
Blueberries	1/2 cup	1/2 cup	3/4 cup

twist & sprout

Breakfast

Get Up & Go French Toast

3 slices thick-cut whole wheat bread
5 eggs
¾ cup 1% or fat-free milk
¾ teaspoon ground cinnamon
2¼ teaspoons sugar
⅛ teaspoon salt

1. Coat a 9 x 13-inch glass dish with non-stick cooking spray. Lay bread slices in the dish.
3. In a bowl, beat eggs well. Stir in milk, cinnamon, sugar and salt.
4. Pour egg mixture over bread and let sit for at least an hour or overnight. Cover and refrigerate to store overnight.
5. Preheat oven to 350 degrees.
6. Bake for about 30 minutes or until golden brown. French toast is done when toothpick comes out clean.
7. Cut in half.

Makes 6 half slices

½ slice provides 0.5 oz. GB and 1 oz. MMA for a 3-5 year old at breakfast

Lunch

Melty Tomato Cheese Sandwich

6 slices whole grain bread
4 tablespoons Dijon mustard
18 slices tomato, ¼-inch thick
9 1-ounce slices mozzarella cheese

1. Preheat broiler.
2. Place bread in a single layer on a baking sheet. Place under broiler until lightly toasted about 1½ minutes per side.
3. Spread 2 teaspoons mustard on each slice of toast. Top each with 3 tomato slices and 1½ slices mozzarella cheese.
4. Return baking sheet to broiler and broil until cheese melts, about 3 minutes.
5. Cut each slice into 2 pieces.

Makes 12 open-faced sandwiches

2 sandwiches provide 1 oz. GB, 1.5 oz. MMA and ¼ cup VEG for a 3-5 year old at lunch

Snack

Butternut Squash Cornbread Muffins

1 14-ounce box enriched honey cornbread mix
1 12-ounce package frozen squash puree, cooked, pureed
⅓ cup 1% or fat-free milk
2 tablespoons butter, melted
1 egg

1. Heat oven to 400 degrees. Line a 12-cup muffin pan with paper liners.
2. In medium bowl, mix all ingredients until blended. Spoon into prepared muffin pan.
3. Bake 16 to 18 minutes.

Makes 12 muffins

½ muffin provides 0.5 oz. GB for a 3-5 year old at snack

Breakfast

Sweet Corn Quesadillas, Milk

	Toddler	Pre-School	School Age
Quesadillas*	1/2 quesadilla	1 quesadilla	1 quesadilla
Milk	1/2 cup	3/4 cup	1 cup

Lunch

Quick Moroccan Chicken, Whole Grain Couscous, Honey-Glazed Carrots, Spinach Salad, Milk

	Toddler	Pre-School	School Age
Chicken*	1/3 cup	1/2 cup	2/3 cup
Couscous	1/4 cup	1/4 cup	1/2 cup
Carrots*	1/8 cup	1/4 cup	1/2 cup
Salad	1/4 cup	1/2 cup	1/2 cup
Milk	1/2 cup	3/4 cup	1 cup

Snack

Peaches, Milk

	Toddler	Pre-School	School Age
Peaches	1/2 cup	1/2 cup	3/4 cup
Milk	1/2 cup	1/2 cup	1 cup

Breakfast

Sweet Corn Quesadillas

6 8-inch corn tortillas
3 teaspoons olive oil
1½ cups Monterey Jack cheese, grated
½ cup red onions, thinly sliced
2 cups whole kernel corn, thawed or drained
½ cup salsa
¼ cup sour cream

1. Preheat oven or toaster oven to 400 degrees. Line a baking sheet with foil.

2. Place tortillas on baking sheet and brush the top side of each tortilla with the oil. Turn 3 of the tortillas over and sprinkle with the cheese, onions and corn. Top with the remaining 3 tortillas, oiled side up.

3. Bake, turning once, until the cheese melts, 6 to 8 minutes total. Cut in half.

4. Serve with sour cream and salsa.

Makes 6 quesadillas

1 quesadilla provides 1 oz. GB., 1 oz. MMA and ½ cup VEG for a 3-5 year old at breakfast

Lunch

Quick Moroccan Chicken

½ cup whole grain couscous
1½ tablespoons olive oil
1 large clove fresh garlic, thinly sliced
¼ cup onions, chopped small
1½ tablespoons light brown sugar
⅛ teaspoon ground nutmeg
1½ tablespoons red wine vinegar
½ cup orange juice
3 cups rotisserie chicken, diced
  (about 1 chicken)
1 15-ounce can diced peaches, drained

1. Cook the couscous according to directions.

2. Meanwhile, in a large skillet, heat the oil over medium-low heat. Add the garlic and onion and cook for 1½ minutes. Then add the sugar, nutmeg, vinegar and orange juice and bring to a simmer.

3. Add the chicken and the peaches. Simmer until liquid has reduced slightly, about 5 minutes.

4. Serve ¼ cup couscous topped with ½ cup of chicken.

Makes about 6 cups

¼ cup couscous and ½ cup of chicken provides 0.5 oz. GB and 1.5 oz. MMA for a 3-5 year old at lunch/supper

Honey-Glazed Carrots

1 tablespoon butter
2 tablespoons honey or brown sugar
¼ cup water
⅛ teaspoon salt
⅛ teaspoon black pepper
4 cups baby carrots

1. In a saucepan, melt the butter over medium heat. Stir in the honey, water, salt and pepper.

2. Add carrots and simmer, partially covered, until carrots are tender, about 12 to 15 minutes.

Makes about 3 cups

½ cup carrots provides ½ cup VEG for a 3-5 year old at lunch/supper

Breakfast

Southwest Breakfast Wraps, Strawberries, Milk

	Toddler	Pre-School	School Age
Breakfast Wraps*	1 wrap	1 wrap	2 wraps
Strawberries	1/4 cup	1/2 cup	1/2 cup
Milk	1/2 cup	3/4 cup	1 cup

Lunch

Ham and Cheese Roll-Ups, Celery, Cucumber Slices, Milk

	Toddler	Pre-School	School Age
Roll-Ups*	2 roll-ups	2 roll-ups	3 roll-ups
Celery	1/8 cup	1/4 cup	1/2 cup
Cucumber	1/8 cup	1/4 cup	1/4 cup
Milk	1/2 cup	3/4 cup	1 cup

Snack

Spiced Chickpeas, Milk

	Toddler	Pre-School	School Age
Spiced Chickpeas*	1/2 cup	1/2 cup	3/4 cup
Milk	1/2 cup	1/2 cup	1 cup

Breakfast

Southwest Breakfast Wraps

6 whole corn tortillas
½ tablespoon olive oil
¼ cup black beans, rinsed and drained
4 eggs, lightly beaten
¼ cup salsa
¼ cup cheese (any type), shredded
⅛ teaspoon salt

1. Turn on oven to 250 degrees. Place tortillas on a baking sheet and place in the oven to warm.

2. In a skillet, heat olive oil over medium heat. Add black beans and sauté for one minute.

3. Add eggs, salsa, shredded cheese and salt. Cook, stirring frequently, until the eggs are set, about 2 to 3 minutes.

4. To serve, spoon a portion of scrambled eggs down the middle of each tortilla and roll up. Then cut in half.

Makes 12 wraps

  1 wrap provides 0.5 oz. GB and
  0.5 oz. MMA for a 3-5 year old at breakfast

Lunch

Ham and Cheese Roll-Ups

1 8-ounce package cream cheese,
  at room temperature
1 ounce grated cheddar cheese,
  at room temperature
9 ounces low-sodium deli ham, chopped
½ cup green onions, thinly sliced
½ cup cucumbers, thinly sliced
6 8-inch whole grain tortillas

1. In medium bowl, mix together cream cheese and cheddar cheese until well combined.

2. Stir in ham, green onions and cucumber.

3. To assemble, spread each tortilla thinly with the ham and cheese spread, leaving ½ inch bare edge on one side. Roll up from other side; cover with plastic wrap and refrigerate.

4. To serve, cut in half.

Makes 12 roll-ups

  2 roll-ups provides 1 oz. GB and
  1.5 oz. MMA for a 3-5 year old
  at lunch/supper

Snack

Spiced Chickpeas

2 tablespoons olive oil
1 teaspoon ground cumin
1 teaspoon garlic powder
1 teaspoon onion powder
1 teaspoon salt
2 15-ounce cans (3 cups) chickpeas,
  rinsed and drained

1. Preheat oven to 400 degrees. Coat a baking sheet with non-stick spray.

2. In a large bowl, stir together the olive oil and spices. Add the chickpeas and toss well.

3. Spread seasoned chickpeas on the baking sheet. Roast in oven until browned, about 20 minutes, stirring occasionally.

Makes 3 cups

  ½ cup provides ½ cup VEG
  for a 3-5 year old at snack

SPRING Week 1 Friday

Breakfast

Blueberry Pancakes, Hard Boiled Eggs, Blueberries, Milk

	Toddler	Pre-School	School Age
Pancakes*	1/2 pancake	1/2 pancake	1 pancake
Eggs	1/2 egg	1/2 egg	1 egg
Blueberries	1/4 cup	1/2 cup	1/2 cup
Milk	1/2 cup	3/4 cup	1 cup

Lunch

Mediterranean Quinoa, Broccoli, Canteloupe, Milk

	Toddler	Pre-School	School Age
Quinoa*	2/3 cup	1 cup	1-1/3 cups
Broccoli	1/8 cup	1/4 cup	1/2 cup
Canteloupe	1/8 cup	1/4 cup	1/4 cup
Milk	1/2 cup	3/4 cup	1 cup

Snack

Creamy Fruit Dip, Apples

	Toddler	Pre-School	School Age
Fruit Dip*	2 tbsp	2 tbsp	4 tbsp
Apples	1/2 cup	1/2 cup	3/4 cup

Breakfast

Blueberry Pancakes

¾ cup whole wheat flour
1 teaspoon baking powder
⅛ teaspoon salt
1 tablespoon butter
1 egg
¾ cup 1% or fat-free milk
½ cup blueberries, washed and drained

1. In a large bowl, sift together the flour, baking powder and salt. Set aside.

2. In a small saucepan, melt the butter.

3. In a medium bowl, whisk the egg, milk and melted butter until well mixed.

4. Add the flour mixture to the egg mixture. Whisk again until blended.

5. Coat a skillet with non-stick spray and heat over medium heat.

6. Spoon batter into the skillet and top each with several blueberries. Cook each side until lightly browned.

Makes 6 pancakes

½ pancake provides 0.5 oz. GB
for a 3-5 year old at breakfast

Lunch

Mediterranean Quinoa

¾ cup quinoa
1½ cups low-sodium vegetable broth
2 tablespoons lemon juice
¾ teaspoon fresh garlic, minced
3 tablespoons olive oil
¾ cup red bell peppers, chopped
⅓ cup green onions, sliced thin
¾ cup cherry tomatoes, halved
2 tablespoons fresh parsley, chopped
2 15-ounce cans (3 cups) white beans (e.g. Great Northern), rinsed and drained
3 ounces feta cheese, crumbled

1. In small saucepan, bring quinoa and broth to a boil. Cover and reduce to a simmer. Cook quinoa for 10 to 15 minutes or until all liquid is absorbed. Set aside to cool.

2. In a small bowl, make dressing by combining lemon juice, garlic and oil. Set aside.

3. When quinoa is cool, place in a large bowl. Add the vegetables, parsley, beans and feta cheese. Pour dressing over all and mix well.

Makes 6 cups

1 cup provides 1 oz. GB and 1.5 oz MMA
for a 3-5 year old at lunch/supper

Snack

Creamy Fruit Dip

¾ cup ricotta cheese
1½ tablespoons strawberry jam

1. In a small bowl, mix ricotta cheese and jam together.

2. Serve with fresh strawberries, chunks of melon, apples or other fruit for dipping.

Makes ¾ cup

2 tablespoons dip provide 0.5 oz. MMA
for a 3-5 year old at snack

Breakfast

Hammy Scrambled Eggs, Whole Grain Toast, Grapes, Milk

	Toddler	Pre-School	School Age
Scrambled Eggs*	1/4 cup	1/4 cup	1/2 cup
Toast	1/2 slice	1/2 slice	1 slice
Grapes	1/4 cup	1/2 cup	1/2 cup
Milk	1/2 cup	3/4 cup	1 cup

Lunch

Toasty Cheesy Bean Sandwiches, Sauteed Parsnips, Mandarin Oranges, Milk

	Toddler	Pre-School	School Age
Sandwiches*	2 sandwiches	2 sandwiches	3 sandwiches
Parsnips*	1/8 cup	1/4 cup	1/2 cup
Oranges	1/8 cup	1/4 cup	1/4 cup
Milk	1/2 cup	3/4 cup	1 cup

Snack

Apple Wedges, String Cheese

	Toddler	Pre-School	School Age
Apple Wedges	1/2 cup	1/2 cup	3/4 cup
String Cheese (1 oz.)	1/2	1/2	1

twist & sprout

Breakfast

Hammy Scrambled Eggs

1½ teaspoons olive oil
3 ounces low-sodium ham, finely chopped
3 eggs, beaten
½ green onion, sliced thin

1. In non-stick skillet, heat oil over medium heat.

2. Add chopped ham and cook, stirring periodically, until ham is lightly browned, about 3 to 5 minutes.

3. Stir in eggs and cook until almost firm to the touch, about 4 minutes. Then add green onions and cook until eggs are firm.

Makes 2 cups

¼ cup provides 0.5 oz. MMA
for a 3-5 year old at breakfast

Lunch

Toasty Cheesy Bean Sandwiches

6 slices whole wheat bread
6 ½-inch slices of tomato
3 cups cooked pinto beans
½ cup barbecue sauce
¾ cup green onions, sliced
1½ cups Parmesan cheese, grated

1. Preheat broiler. Line two baking sheets with parchment paper.

2. Place bread slices on one baking sheet. Place tomatoes on the other baking sheet and place it under the broiler. Broil until tomatoes start to wilt or brown, about 3 to 5 minutes.

3. Meanwhile, in a small bowl, mix together the beans and barbecue sauce.

4. Remove tomatoes from broiler, set aside.

5. To assemble, spoon a heaping ⅓ cup of beans over each bread slice. Top with 1 broiled tomato slice, a sprinkle of green onions and ¼ cup Parmesan cheese.

6. Place sandwiches under broiler until cheese bubbles and browns, about 3 minutes.

7. To serve, cut in half.

Makes 12 open-faced sandwiches

2 sandwiches provide 1 oz. GB and 1.5 oz. MMA
for a 3-5 year old at lunch/supper

Lunch

Sauteed Parsnips

1½ teaspoons olive oil
1½ pounds (3 cups) parsnips,
   peeled and sliced thin
¼ teaspoon salt
¼ teaspoon parsley, dried

1. In a large skillet, heat oil over medium heat.

2. Add parsnips and salt, and stir. Cook until almost tender and lightly golden in color, about 7-10 minutes.

3. Add the parsley and cook until tender, about 1 to 2 more minutes.

Makes 3 cups

¼ cup provides ¼ cup VEG
for a 3-5 year old at lunch/supper

Breakfast

Apple Z Muffins, Orange Wedges, Milk

	Toddler	Pre-School	School Age
Muffin*	1/2 muffin	1/2 muffin	1 muffins
Oranges	1/4 cup	1/2 cup	1/2 cup
Milk	1/2 cup	3/4 cup	1 cup

Lunch

Creamy Carrot Soup, Whole Grain Crackers, Cheese, Blueberries, Milk

	Toddler	Pre-School	School Age
Carrot Soup*	1/4 cup	1/2 cup	1 cup
Crackers	3	3	6
Cheese	1 oz.	1.5 oz.	2 oz.
Blueberries	1/8 cup	1/4 cup	1/4 cup
Milk	1/2 cup	3/4 cup	1 cup

Snack

Banana-Strawberry Hats, Milk

	Toddler	Pre-School	School Age
Hats*	2 hats	2 hats	3 hats
Milk	1/2 cup	1/2 cup	1 cup

Breakfast

Apple Z Muffins

1½ cups whole wheat flour
½ cup brown sugar
1½ teaspoons baking soda
1½ teaspoons ground cinnamon
¼ teaspoon allspice
¼ teaspoon salt
1½ cups zucchini, grated
1¼ cups apples, peeled, cored and grated
2 eggs
1 teaspoon vanilla
⅓ cup unsweetened applesauce
⅓ cup canola oil

1. Preheat oven to 350 degrees. Coat two 6-cup muffin pans with non-stick spray.

2. In a large bowl, mix together flour, brown sugar, baking soda, cinnamon, allspice and salt. Stir in the zucchini and apples.

3. In a separate bowl, combine eggs, vanilla, applesauce and oil. Pour the eggs into the flour mixture and stir until just mixed.

4. Spoon into muffin pan. Bake for 20 minutes.

Makes 12 small muffins

 ½ muffin provides 0.5 oz. GB
 for a 3-5 year old at breakfast

Lunch

Creamy Carrot Soup

2 teaspoons olive oil
⅓ cup onions, chopped
1½ pounds carrots, sliced
3 cups low-sodium vegetable broth
2 teaspoons ginger, grated
1 teaspoon salt
⅛ teaspoon black pepper
⅓ cup 1% or fat-free milk
2 teaspoons dried dill

1. In a large saucepan, heat the oil over medium-high heat. Add the onions and carrots and cook 5 to 6 minutes.

2. Add broth, ginger, salt and pepper. Bring to a boil and then reduce heat.

3. Add milk and dill. Simmer until carrots are soft, about 15 to 20 minutes.

4. Using an immersion blender or regular blender, puree the soup in batches until smooth.

Makes 6 cups

 ½ cup provides ¼ cup VEG
 for a 3-5 year old at lunch/supper

Snack

Banana-Strawberry Hats

1 pint large strawberries, washed and hulled
3 large bananas

1. Slice strawberries crosswise.

2. Slice bananas crosswise.

3. Stack 4 slices each of strawberry and banana, alternating them to look like Dr. Suess's *Cat in the Hat* hats.

Makes 12 "hats"

 2 hats provide ½ cup FR
 for a 3-5 year old at snack

Breakfast

Pretty Parfait, Milk

	Toddler	Pre-School	School Age
Parfait	1/2 parfait	1 parfait	1 parfait
Milk	1/2 cup	3/4 cup	1 cup

Lunch

Tasty Tacos, Corn, Grapes, Milk

	Toddler	Pre-School	School Age
Tacos*	1/2 taco	1 taco	1 taco
Corn	1/8 cup	1/4 cup	1/2 cup
Grapes	1/8 cup	1/4 cup	1/4 cup
Milk	1/2 cup	3/4 cup	1 cup

Snack

Black Bean Dip, Red Pepper Strips

	Toddler	Pre-School	School Age
Dip*	2 tbsp	2 tbsp	4 tbsp
Red Pepper	1/2 cup	1/2 cup	3/4 cup

Breakfast

Pretty Parfait

3 cups pineapple, drained and chopped
3 cups plain low-fat yogurt
2 cups granola
3 strawberries, washed, hulled and sliced

1. In individual glasses or bowls, spoon ½ cup pineapple to form the parfait's bottom layer.
2. Layer ½ cup yogurt on top of the pineapple.
3. Layer ⅓ cup granola on top of the yogurt.
4. Garnish each parfait with a few slices of strawberry.

Makes 6 parfaits

  1 parfait provides 1 oz. GB and ½ cup FR for a 3-5 year old at breakfast

Lunch

Tasty Tacos

2 teaspoons vegetable oil
1 pound ground beef (85/15)
½ cup onions, chopped
¾ ounce taco seasoning (½ package)
⅓ cup salsa
¼ cup water
6 8-inch whole grain tortillas
1½ cups lettuce, shredded
1 avocado, pitted, peeled and chopped
½ cup salsa
½ cup cheese, finely shredded

1. In large skillet, heat oil over medium heat. Add onions and ground beef and sauté until beef is thoroughly cooked, about 8 to 10 minutes.
2. Stir in taco seasoning, salsa and water.
3. Reduce heat to low. Simmer until most of the liquid is absorbed, about 8 to 10 minutes.
4. Serve cooked meat with tortillas and lettuce, avocado, salsa and cheese for toppings.

Makes 6 tacos

  1 taco provides 1 oz. GB, 2 oz. MMA and ¼ cup VEG for a 3-5 year old at lunch/supper

Snack

Black Bean Dip

1 15-ounce can (1½ cups) black beans, rinsed and drained
1 teaspoon pickled jalapenos, chopped
1 tablespoon fresh cilantro, chopped
2 teaspoons lemon juice
2 teaspoons olive oil
½ teaspoon fresh garlic, chopped
3 cups red bell peppers, sliced

1. Place all ingredients, except the peppers, into a food processor. Process until smooth, about 1 to 2 minutes. Dip will be thick and creamy.
2. Serve with ½ cup red bell pepper slices.

Makes 1½ cups dip

  2 tablespoons dip and ½ cup red bell peppers provide 0.5 oz. MMA and ½ cup VEG for a 3-5 year old at snack

SPRING **Week 2** Thursday

Breakfast

Breakfast Sandwich, Apple Fans, Milk

	Toddler	Pre-School	School Age
Sandwich*	1/2 sandwich	1/2 sandwich	1 sandwich
Apples	1/4 cup	1/2 cup	1/2 cup
Milk	1/2 cup	3/4 cup	1 cup

Lunch

Teriyaki Turkey Burger on Whole Grain Bun, Baked Beans, Peaches, Milk

	Toddler	Pre-School	School Age
Burger*	1/2 burger	1 burger	1 burger
Baked Beans	1/8 cup	1/4 cup	1/2 cup
Peaches	1/8 cup	1/4 cup	1/4 cup
Milk	1/2 cup	3/4 cup	1 cup

Snack

Parmesan Zucchini Crisps, Milk

	Toddler	Pre-School	School Age
Crisps*	8	8	12
Milk	1/2 cup	1/2 cup	1 cup

twist & sprout

 **SPRING Week 2** Thursday

Breakfast

Breakfast Sandwich

3 whole grain English muffins, split and toasted
3 eggs, scrambled
6 tablespoons cheddar cheese, grated

1. Lightly toast muffin halves in toaster or under the broiler.
2. Scramble eggs in skillet or in microwave.
3. To assemble, portion scrambled egg and cheese onto three muffin halves and top with remaining muffins halves.
4. Heat sandwiches in a 300 degree oven until cheese is melted, about 5 minutes.
5. To serve, cut in half.

Makes 3 sandwiches

½ sandwich provides 1 oz. GB and
0.5 oz. MMA for a 3-5 year old at breakfast

Lunch

Teriyaki Turkey Burger

1¼ pounds ground turkey
¼ teaspoon ground ginger
¼ teaspoon garlic powder
½ teaspoon salt
¼ teaspoon pepper
¼ cup low-sodium teriyaki sauce
6 whole grain buns
1 cup cucumbers, sliced

1. Heat grill or grill pan over medium-high heat.
2. In bowl, mix turkey with ginger, garlic, salt and pepper. Form into 6 ½-inch thick patties.
3. Cook burgers until firm to the touch, about 6 to 8 minutes per side for well done or until internal temperature reaches 165 degrees.
4. Baste with the teriyaki sauce during the last 2 minutes of cooking.
5. Place burger in bun and top with cucumber slices.

Makes 6 burgers

1 burger with bun provides 1 oz. GB and
2 oz. MMA for a 3-5 year old at lunch/supper

Snack

Parmesan Zucchini Crisps

1½ pounds zucchini (2 large or 4 medium)
2 eggs, beaten
⅔ cup Italian dressing
2 cups breadcrumbs
1 teaspoon basil
1 teaspoon oregano
1 cup Parmesan cheese, grated

1. Preheat oven to 450 degrees. Line baking sheets with foil and coat with non-stick spray.
2. Slice zucchini into thin rounds.
3. In a bowl, beat eggs with the Italian dressing.
4. In a separate bowl, combine breadcrumbs, basil, oregano, and Parmesan cheese.
5. First, dip the zucchini rounds in the dressing and then dredge in the breadcrumbs. Place on baking sheets.
6. Bake until golden brown and crispy, about 20 minutes.

Makes 3 cups

8 crisps provide ½ cup VEG
for a 3-5 year old at snack

SPRING Week 2 Friday

Breakfast

Sweetheart Pancakes with Strawberry Compote, Milk

	Toddler	Pre-School	School Age
Pancakes*	1/2 pancake	1 pancake	1 pancake
Strawberry Compote*	1/4 cup	1/2 cup	1/2 cup
Milk	1/2 cup	3/4 cup	1 cup

Lunch

Chicken Stir-Fry, Savory Brown Rice, Celery, Peppy Pineapple, Milk

	Toddler	Pre-School	School Age
Stir-Fry*	1/2 cup	3/4 cup	1 cup
Brown Rice*	1/4 cup	1/4 cup	1/2 cup
Celery	1/8 cup	1/4 cup	1/4 cup
Pineapple	1/8 cup	1/4 cup	1/4 cup
Milk	1/2 cup	3/4 cup	1 cup

Snack

String Cheese, Broccoli Trees

	Toddler	Pre-School	School Age
Cheese	1/2 piece	1/2 piece	1 piece
Broccoli	1/2 cup	1/2 cup	3/4 cup

Breakfast

Sweetheart Pancakes with Strawberry Compote

3 cups strawberries, washed, hulled and sliced
1 tablespoon sugar
1 teaspoon lemon juice
6 pancakes, cooked

1. Combine strawberries, sugar and lemon juice in a bowl.

2. Prepare pancakes or warm, pre-cooked pancakes in 350 degree oven.

3. Serve each pancake with ½ cup compote.

Makes 6 pancakes and 3 cups compote

1 pancake with ½ cup compote provides 1 oz. GB and ½ cup FR for a 3-5 year old at breakfast

Lunch

Chicken Stir-Fry

1 tablespoon vegetable oil
½ cup sweet onions, sliced
1 pound boneless chicken breast, cut into bite-sized pieces
¾ cup low-sodium teriyaki marinade
½ tablespoon fresh garlic, minced
1½ cups broccoli, chopped
1 cup bell peppers, chunked

1. In large skillet, heat the oil over medium-high heat.

2. Add onions and chicken. Cook 2 minutes, stirring often. Stir in teriyaki marinade and garlic.

3. Add broccoli and peppers. Cook 5-7 minutes. Cover to speed up cooking. When chicken is cooked through, remove from heat.

Makes 4½ cups

¾ cup provides 1.5 oz. MMA and ¼ cup VEG for a 3-5 year old at lunch/supper

Lunch

Savory Brown Rice

1 cup parboiled brown rice
¼ teaspoon salt (optional)
2 cups low-sodium vegetable or chicken broth

1. In medium saucepan add brown rice, salt and broth. Bring to boil, cover and reduce heat to a simmer.

2. Simmer until all the water has been absorbed and rice is tender, about 30 minutes.

3. Remove from heat and let stand, covered, for 5-10 minutes before serving.

Makes 3 cups

¼ cup rice provides 0.5 oz. GB for a 3-5 year old at lunch/supper

Breakfast

Green Egg Popper, Whole Grain Toast, Peaches, Milk

	Toddler	Pre-School	School Age
Poppers*	1/2 popper	1 popper	1 popper
Toast	1/2 slice	1/2 slice	1 slice
Peaches	1/4 cup	1/2 cup	1/2 cup
Milk	1/2 cup	3/4 cup	1 cup

Lunch

Black Bean Taco Salad, Whole Grain Corn Chips, Grapes, Milk

	Toddler	Pre-School	School Age
Salad*	1/2 cup	3/4 cup	1 cup
Spinach	1/2 cup	3/4 cup	1 cup
Corn Chips	5	5	10
Grapes	1/8 cup	1/4 cup	1/4 cup
Milk	1/2 cup	3/4 cup	1 cup

Snack

Creamy Zucchini Crackers

	Toddler	Pre-School	School Age
Crackers*	5	5	8

twist & sprout

38

Breakfast

Green Egg Poppers

1½ tablespoons unsalted butter
2 tablespoons green onions, sliced
2 cups kale, finely chopped, loosely packed
3 large eggs
1½ cups cooked potatoes, diced small
¼ cup shredded mozzarella cheese

1. Preheat oven to 400 degrees. Coat a 6-muffin pan with non-stick cooking spray.

2. In a large skillet, heat butter over medium-high heat. Add green onions and kale. Cook until tender and water evaporates, about 5 minutes. Remove from heat; set aside to cool.

3. In a large bowl, lightly beat the eggs. Add the cooked kale, potatoes and cheese to the eggs and season with salt and pepper.

4. Spoon batter into muffin pan and bake in oven until eggs poppers are firm, about 13-15 minutes.

Makes 6 poppers

  1 popper provides 1 oz. MMA and
  ½ cup VEG for a 3-5 year old at breakfast

Lunch

Black Bean Taco Salad

1½ 15-ounce cans (2 cups) black beans, rinsed and drained
1½ cups tomatoes, chopped
¼ cup green onions, chopped
½ cup cheddar cheese, shredded
2 tablespoons lemon juice
1 teaspoon ground cumin
¼ teaspoon pepper
4 cups fresh spinach, chopped

1. In a large bowl, combine beans, tomatoes, onions and cheese.

2. In a small bowl, mix lemon juice, cumin and pepper. Pour over beans and toss.

3. To serve, make bed of ¾ cup spinach and spoon taco salad on top.

Makes 4½ cups

  ¾ cup of taco salad and ¾ cup spinach
  provide 1.5 oz. MMA and ½ cup VEG for a
  3-5 year old at lunch/supper

Snack

Creamy Zucchini Crackers

2 cups zucchini, cut into rounds
1½ tablespoons olive oil
1½ cups hummus
30 small whole grain crackers (like Triscuits)

1. Preheat oven to 400 degrees. Line a baking sheet with foil or parchment.

2. Cut zucchini into thin rounds. In a bowl, toss zucchini with the olive oil. Spread in a single layer on baking sheet.

3. Bake until lightly browned and tender, about 10 minutes.

3. To assemble, top each cracker with ½ tablespoon hummus and 1 tablespoon zucchini slices.

Makes 30 crackers

  5 crackers provide 1 oz. GB and
  ½ cup VEG for a 3-5 year old at snack

Breakfast

Breakfast Frushi, Milk

	Toddler	Pre-School	School Age
Frushi*	2	4	4
Milk	1/2 cup	3/4 cup	1 cup

Lunch

Cheesy Chicken Pizza, Green Beans, Apple Slices, Milk

	Toddler	Pre-School	School Age
Pizza*	1 pizza	1 pizza	2 pizzas
Green Beans	1/8 cup	1/4 cup	1/2 cup
Apple Slices	1/8 cup	1/4 cup	1/4 cup
Milk	1/2 cup	3/4 cup	1 cup

Snack

Strawberry-Kiwi Salsa, Whole Grain Tortilla Crisps

	Toddler	Pre-School	School Age
Salsa*	1/2 cup	1/2 cup	3/4 cup
Tortillla Crisps	3	3	6

40

 **SPRING Week 3** Tuesday

Breakfast

Breakfast Frushi

6 medium bananas, peeled
12 tablespoons peanut butter
4 cups crisp rice cereal

1. Spread 2 tablespoons peanut butter on each banana.
2. Roll each banana in ⅔ cup cereal. Slice each banana into 4 "frushi" rolls.

Makes 24 frushi rolls

 4 frushi provide 1 oz. GB, 1 oz. MMA and ½ cup FR for a 3-5 year old at breakfast

Lunch

Cheesy Chicken Pizza

3 1-oz. whole grain bagels, cut in half
¾ cup low-sodium marinara sauce
6 ounce cooked chicken breast, shredded
1½ cups mozzarella cheese, grated

1. Preheat broiler.
2. Place bagels, cut side up, on a baking sheet. Broil until lightly toasted, about 2 minutes, and remove from oven.
3. On each bagel half, spread 2 tablespoons marinara sauce. Top each with ¼ cup chicken and sprinkle with ¼ cup cheese.
4. Broil pizzas until cheese melts, about 2 minutes.

Makes 6 pizzas

 1 pizza provides 1 oz. GB and 1.5 oz. MMA for a 3-5 year old at lunch/supper

Snack

Strawberry-Kiwi Salsa

2 medium Granny Smith apples
1 kiwi fruit, peeled
1 cup strawberries
1 orange, peeled
2 tablespoons jelly
2 tablespoons brown sugar (optional)
4 8-inch whole wheat tortillas
2 tablespoons sugar
2 tablespoons ground cinnamon
water

1. Finely chop all fruit. Mix together with sugar and jelly.
2. To make the crisps, mix sugar and cinnamon together in a small bowl. Lightly brush tortillas with water and then sprinkle with the cinnamon/sugar mixture.
3. Cut each tortilla into 6 wedges and bake at 350 degrees until golden brown, about 5-7 minutes.

Makes 4 cups salsa, 24 crisps

 ½ cup salsa and 3 tortilla crisps provide 1 oz. GB and ½ cup FR for a 3-5 year old at snack

Breakfast

Berry Nice Oatmeal, Milk

	Toddler	Pre-School	School Age
Oatmeal*	1/4 cup	1/4 cup	1/2 cup
Berries	1/4 cup	1/2 cup	1/2 cup
Milk	1/2 cup	3/4 cup	1 cup

Lunch

Broccoli-Beef Bowl, Brown Rice, Mandarin Oranges, Milk

	Toddler	Pre-School	School Age
Broccoli-Beef Bowl*	1/2 cup	3/4 cup	1 cup
Brown Rice	1/4 cup	1/4 cup	1/2 cup
Mandarin Oranges	1/8 cup	1/4 cup	1/4 cup
Milk	1/2 cup	3/4 cup	1 cup

Snack

Yummy Yams, Milk

	Toddler	Pre-School	School Age
Yams*	1/2 cup	1/2 cup	3/4 cup
Milk	1/2 cup	1/2 cup	1 cup

Breakfast

Berry Nice Oatmeal

1½ cups water
¾ cup regular rolled oats
½ teaspoon ground cinnamon
1½ cups strawberries, washed, hulled
  and finely chopped
1½ cups blueberries

1. In medium saucepan, bring water and oats to boil. Add cinnamon.

2. Simmer oats for 10 minutes or until thickened and tender.

3. Top each portion with ¼ cup of strawberries and ¼ cup of blueberries.

Makes 1½ cups

¼ cup oatmeal with ½ cup berries provides 0.5 oz. GB and ½ cup FR for a 3-5 year old at breakfast

Lunch

Broccoli-Beef Bowl

¾ cup brown rice, parboiled or instant
1½ cups water
3 tablespoons low-sodium soy sauce
2 teaspoons cornstarch
1½ teaspoons olive oil
1 pound ground beef (85/15)
¾ cup onions, sliced
1½ cups carrots, chopped small
3½ cups broccoli florets

1. Cook rice according to package directions.

2. In a small bowl, whisk together soy sauce and cornstarch and set aside.

3. Heat oil in a large skillet over medium heat. Add beef to skillet and cook until browned, stirring regularly, about 2 minutes.

4. Add onions, carrots and broccoli to skillet and cook until broccoli is crisp-tender, stirring occasionally. Add soy sauce to pan. Bring to a boil and simmer until thick, about 2 minutes.

5. To serve, place ¼ cup rice in bowl and top with ¾ cup broccoli-beef mixture.

Makes 4½ cups

¼ cup rice and ¾ cup broccoli-beef provides 0.5 oz. GB, 1.5 oz MMA and ½ cup VEG for a 3-5 year old at lunch/supper

Snack

Yummy Yams

2 pounds yams, peeled and cut into sticks
¼ cup olive oil
½ teaspoon salt
1 tablespoon brown sugar
2 tablespoons Parmesan cheese, grated

1. Preheat oven to 450 degrees. Line a baking sheet with foil or parchment paper. Coat with non-stick cooking spray.

2. In a large bowl, toss the yams with the olive oil. Sprinkle with the salt, sugar and Parmesan cheese and mix thoroughly.

3. Spread seasoned yams in a single layer on the baking sheet.

4. Bake for 20 to 30 minutes. Stir after 15 minutes and continue cooking until they are browned.

5. Cool 5 minutes before serving.

Makes about 3 cups

½ cup provides ½ cup VEG for a 3-5 year old at snack

Breakfast

Good Morning Sunshine, Milk

	Toddler	Pre-School	School Age
Yogurt*	1/4 cup	1/4 cup	1/2 cup
Granola*	1/8 cup	1/8 cup	1/4 cup
Oranges*	1/4 cup	1/4 cup	1/2 cup
Milk	1/2 cup	3/4 cup	1 cup

Lunch

Crazy Quinoa, Corn, Strawberries, Milk

	Toddler	Pre-School	School Age
Quinoa*	1/2 cup	3/4 cup	1 cup
Corn	1/8 cup	1/4 cup	1/2 cup
Strawberries	1/8 cup	1/4 cup	1/4 cup
Milk	1/2 cup	3/4 cup	1 cup

Snack

Edamame Dip, Vegetable Sticks, Toast Triangles

	Toddler	Pre-School	School Age
Dip*	1/4 cup	1/4 cup	1/4 cup
Vegetable Sticks	1/4 cup	1/4 cup	1/2 cup
Toast Triangles*	2 triangles	2 triangles	4 triangles

Breakfast

Good Morning Sunshine

3 cups fresh orange slices
1½ cups low-fat yogurt, any flavor
¾ cup granola, any flavor

1. On each plate, arrange ½ cup orange slices in a circle to make "sunshine."
2. In the middle of the oranges, spoon ¼ cup yogurt and top with ⅛ cup granola.

Makes 6 sunshines

1 sunshine provides 0.5 oz. GB, 0.5 oz. MMA and ½ cup FR for a 3-5 year old at breakfast

Lunch

Crazy Quinoa

¾ cup quinoa
2 cups low-sodium vegetable broth
3 cups cooked chicken, cut into bite-sized pieces
4 tablespoons olive oil
½ cup green onions, chopped
1½ cups cherry tomatoes, halved
½ cup Parmesan cheese, grated

1. In saucepan, bring quinoa and broth to a boil. Cover and reduce to a simmer. Cook quinoa for 10-15 minutes or until all liquid is absorbed.
2. In a large bowl, mix together the hot quinoa with the cooked chicken, olive oil, green onion, cherry tomatoes and Parmesan cheese. Serve hot.

Makes 5½ cups

¾ cup provides 1 oz. GB, 1.5 oz. MMA and ¼ cup VEG for a 3-5 year old at lunch/supper

Snack

Edamame Dip & Toast Triangles

3 slices whole grain bread, toasted and cut into quarters
3 cups frozen shelled edamame (soybeans)
¼ teaspoon garlic powder
¾ cup plain low-fat yogurt
3 tablespoons lemon juice
1½ tablespoons olive oil
¼ teaspoon salt
¼ teaspoon pepper
1½ cups assorted vegetable sticks for dipping

1. Prepare soybeans according to package directions.
2. Place cooked edamame and remaining ingredients, except vegetable sticks, into a food processor. Pulse until smooth.
3. Serve with carrot, celery or jicama sticks for dipping and with toast triangles on the side.

Makes 3½ cups

¼ cup dip, ¼ cup vegetable sticks and 2 toast triangles provide 0.5 oz. GB and ½ cup VEG for a 3-5 year old at snack

Breakfast

Blueberry Crepes, Milk

	Toddler	Pre-School	School Age
Crepes*	1/2 crepe	1 crepe	1 crepe
Milk	1/2 cup	3/4 cup	1 cup

Lunch

Spicy Shredded Beef on Whole Grain Bun, Peas, Cantaloupe, Milk

	Toddler	Pre-School	School Age
Shredded Beef*	1/3 cup	1/2 cup	2/3 cup
Bun	1/2 bun	1/2 bun	1 bun
Peas	1/8 cup	1/4 cup	1/2 cup
Cantaloupe	1/8 cup	1/4 cup	1/4 cup
Milk	1/2 cup	3/4 cup	1 cup

Snack

Cinnamon Apples, Cottage Cheese

	Toddler	Pre-School	School Age
Cinnamon Apples*	1/2 cup	1/2 cup	3/4 cup
Cottage Cheese	1/8 cup	1/8 cup	1/4 cup

Breakfast

Easy Blueberry Crepes

3 cups whole wheat flour
¼ teaspoon salt
3¾ cups 1% or fat-free milk
6 eggs, at room temperature
¼ cup butter, melted
3 cups blueberries

1. Put all ingredients, except blueberries, in blender and mix well. Let stand for at least 5 minutes and then blend again for about 5 seconds.

2. Preheat non-stick skillet on medium heat until hot. Add a little butter or oil, if desired, to coat the pan.

3. Pour ½ cup of the crepe batter into the skillet and quickly swirl batter around to cover the bottom of the pan in a thin layer. Cook crepe until the top looks dry and the edges are cooked and firm, about 3 minutes. When crepe is firm but pliable, remove from heat.

4. Top with ½ cup blueberries and roll up. Cut in half to serve.

Makes 12 crepes

2 crepes provide 1 oz. GB, 1 oz. MMA and ½ cup FR for a 3-5 year old at breakfast

Lunch

Spicy Shredded Beef

7 ounces canned diced tomatoes
½ cup salsa
½ onion, chopped
1½ cloves fresh garlic, minced
1 tablespoon chili powder
1½ tablespoons honey
1¼ teaspoons salt
½ teaspoon ground cumin
1 cup low-sodium beef broth
1 pound boneless beef chuck roast
6 whole grain hamburger buns

1. Coat a 5 quart or larger slow cooker with non-stick spray.

2. In a bowl, whisk together all the ingredients except the beef and buns.

3. Place beef on the bottom of the slow cooker, followed by the rest of the ingredients.

4. Cover and cook on low until beef is very tender when pierced, about 8 hours. If desired, remove lid for the last 30 minutes to allow sauce to reduce and thicken.

5. When done, use a heavy fork to transfer meat to a rimmed board or plate. Shred with two forks.

6. To serve, place ½ cup of the beef on a bun, one slice of tomato and the top half of the bun.

Makes 3 cups

½ cup meat on a bun provides 1 oz. GB and 1.5 oz. MMA for a 3-5 year old at lunch/supper

Snack

Cinnamon Apples

3 cups apples, cored and diced
1½ teaspoons lemon juice
3 cups water
½ teaspoon ground cinnamon

1. In a bowl, mix the water and lemon juice. As you dice the apples, place them in the lemon water to prevent browning. Remove apples from water, drain and pat dry.

2. In a medium bowl, sprinkle cinnamon over the apples and toss until evenly distributed.

Makes 3 cups

½ cup of cinnamon apples provides ½ cup FR for a 3-5 year old at snack

Breakfast

PBJ Roll-Ups, Cantaloupe Bites, Milk

	Toddler	Pre-School	School Age
Roll-Ups*	2 roll-ups	2 roll-ups	4 roll-ups
Cantaloupe	1/4 cup	1/2 cup	1/2 cup
Milk	1/2 cup	3/4 cup	1 cup

Lunch

Inside-Out Roast Beef Sandwich, Summertime Carrots, Peppy Pineapple, Milk

	Toddler	Pre-School	School Age
Beef Sandwich*	1 sandwich	1 sandwich	2 sandwiches
Carrots*	1/8 cup	1/4 cup	1/2 cup
Pineapple	1/8 cup	1/4 cup	1/4 cup
Milk	1/2 cup	3/4 cup	1 cup

Snack

Strawberries, Milk

	Toddler	Pre-School	School Age
Strawberries	1/2 cup	1/2 cup	3/4 cup
Milk	1/2 cup	1/2 cup	1 cup

Breakfast

PBJ Roll-Ups

3 slices whole grain bread
3 tablespoons natural nut butter
3 tablespoons natural jam or preserves

1. Remove crusts from bread. Flatten the bread by using a rolling pin, can or bottle

2. Spread ½ tablespoon of nut butter and ½ tablespoon of jam on each slice of bread.

3. Roll up each slice tightly and cut into 4 pieces.

Makes 12 roll-ups

2 roll-ups provide 0.5 oz. GB
for a 3-5 year old at breakfast

Lunch

Inside-Out Roast Beef Sandwich

3 slices whole grain bread, cut in half
1 tablespoon prepared mustard
6 ounces low-sodium deli roast beef
3 1-ounce slices cheddar cheese, cut in half
¾ cup fresh spinach
¾ cup tomatoes, sliced
6 cucumber slices

1. Spread mustard on one side of each half-slice of bread.

2. Lay slices of roast beef on a plate and top each with a half-slice of cheese.

3. Place bread on top of the cheese and then roll up with the roast beef on the outside and the bread in the middle.

4. Top with spinach, tomato and cucumber and secure with toothpick. Remove the toothpick before serving.

Makes 6 sandwiches

1 sandwich provides 0.5 oz. GB,
1.5 oz. MMA and ¼ cup VEG for a 3-5 year
old at lunch/supper

Lunch

Summertime Carrots

4 cups carrots, peeled and chunked
1½ tablespoons olive oil
¼ teaspoon dried thyme
¼ teaspoon dried dill
¼ teaspoon salt

1. Preheat oven to 350 degrees. Line baking sheet with foil or parchment.

2. Place carrots in a bowl and toss with the oil. Sprinkle on the spices and mix well.

3. Place carrots on baking sheet in a single layer and roast until lightly golden and tender, but not mushy, about 20 to 30 minutes,

Makes 3 cups

¼ cup carrots provides ¼ cup VEG
for a 3-5 year old at lunch/supper

SPRING Week 4 Tuesday

Breakfast

Banana Bread, Banana Wheels, Milk

	Toddler	Pre-School	School Age
Banana Bread*	1/2 slice	1/2 slice	1 slice
Bananas	1/4 cup	1/2 cup	1/2 cup
Milk	1/2 cup	3/4 cup	1 cup

Lunch

Chicken Pizza Puffs, Spinach Salad, Grapes, Milk

	Toddler	Pre-School	School Age
Pizza Puffs*	1 puff	1 puff	2 puffs
Spinach Salad	1/4 cup	1/2 cup	1 cup
Grapes	1/8 cup	1/4 cup	1/4 cup
Milk	1/2 cup	3/4 cup	1 cup

Snack

Zucchini Chips, Whole Grain Crackers

	Toddler	Pre-School	School Age
Zucchini Chips*	8	8	12
Crackers	3	3	6

Breakfast

Banana Bread

2 eggs
½ cup applesauce
½ cup brown sugar
1¼ cups bananas, mashed
2 cups whole wheat flour
2 teaspoons baking powder
¼ teaspoon baking soda
½ teaspoon salt
¼ teaspoon ground cinnamon

1. Preheat the oven to 350 degrees. Grease a standard loaf pan and set aside.

2. In a large bowl, beat eggs well. Stir in the applesauce, sugar and mashed bananas.

3. In a separate bowl, sift together the flour, baking powder, baking soda, salt and cinnamon.

4. Add wet mixture to the dry mixture and mix well. Pour batter into the loaf pan.

5. Bake for 50-70 minutes.

6. When ready to serve, cut into 16 slices.

Makes 16 slices

½ slice provides 0.5 oz. GB
for a 3-5 year old at breakfast

Lunch

Chicken Pizza Puffs

½ cup whole wheat flour
½ teaspoon baking powder
½ cup 1% or fat-free milk
1 egg, lightly beaten
½ cup mozzarella cheese, shredded
½ cup broccoli, thawed and finely chopped
9 ounces cooked chicken, finely chopped
12 ounces low-sodium marinara sauce

1. Preheat the oven to 375 degrees. Coat a 12-cup muffin pan with non-stick cooking spray.

2. In a large bowl, whisk together the flour and baking powder. Whisk in the milk and egg.

3. Stir in mozzarella, broccoli and chicken and mix well. Spoon into the muffin pan.

5. Bake until puffed, golden and firm to the touch, about 20 to 25 minutes.

6. While baking, warm the marinara sauce in a saucepan.

7. Serve each pizza puff with ¼ cup marinara sauce.

Makes 6 pizza puffs

1 puff provides 0.5 oz. GB, 1.5 oz MMA and ¼ cup VEG for a 3-5 year old at lunch/supper

Snack

Zucchini Chips

⅓ cup breadcrumbs
¼ teaspoon salt
½ teaspoon dried basil
½ teaspoon dried thyme
¾ teaspoon garlic powder
¼ teaspoon freshly ground black pepper
¼ cup 1% or fat-free milk
4 cups zucchini, sliced ¼" thick

1. Preheat oven to 450 degrees. Line a baking sheet with foil and coat a wire rack with non-stick cooking spray.

2. In a bowl, whisk together breadcrumbs with all the spices.

3. Place milk in a shallow bowl. Dip zucchini slices in milk and then dredge in the seasoned breadcrumbs.

4. Place zucchini slices on the wire rack and place the rack on the baking sheet.

5. Bake until browned and crisp, about 20 to 30 minutes.

Makes 6 servings

8 chips provide ½ cup VEG
for a 3-5 year old at snack

Breakfast

Sweet Quinoa, Scrambled Eggs, Strawberries, Milk

	Toddler	Pre-School	School Age
Quinoa*	1/4 cup	1/4 cup	1/2 cup
Eggs	1/4 cup	1/4 cup	1/2 cup
Strawberries	1/4 cup	1/2 cup	1/2 cup
Milk	1/2 cup	3/4 cup	1 cup

Lunch

Taco-Style Lentils and Rice, Peas, Mandarin Oranges, Milk

	Toddler	Pre-School	School Age
Lentils and Rice*	3/4 cup	3/4 cup	1-1/2 cup
Peas	1/8 cup	1/4 cup	1/2 cup
Mandarin Oranges	1/8 cup	1/4 cup	1/4 cup
Milk	1/2 cup	3/4 cup	1 cup

Snack

Carrot Fries, Milk

	Toddler	Pre-School	School Age
Carrot Fries*	1/2 cup	1/2 cup	3/4 cup
Milk	1/2 cup	1/2 cup	1 cup

twist & sprout

52

Breakfast

Sweet Quinoa

1½ cups water
¾ cup quinoa
½ teaspoon ground cinnamon
3 cups strawberries, washed, hulled and sliced
6 tablespoons walnuts, chopped
Honey or brown sugar to taste

1. In a medium saucepan, bring water and quinoa to a boil. Add cinnamon, then cover and reduce heat to a simmer.

2. Simmer until water is absorbed and quinoa is tender, about 12-15 minutes.

3. To serve, top quinoa with sliced strawberries, walnuts and honey or brown sugar.

Makes 1½ cups

¼ cup quinoa and ½ cup berries provide 0.5 oz. GB and ½ cup FR for a 3-5 year old at breakfast

Lunch

Taco-Style Lentils and Rice

4 cups low-sodium beef or chicken broth
¾ cup dry lentils
¾ cup parboiled brown rice
2 teaspoons chili powder
1 teaspoon cumin ground
¾ teaspoon onion powder
½ teaspoon garlic powder
2 cups romaine lettuce, shredded
1 cup tomatoes, diced
¾ cup cheddar cheese, grated

1. In medium saucepan, bring broth, lentils, rice and spices to a boil. Cover and reduce to a simmer.

2. Simmer until lentils and rice are tender, about 30 to 45 minutes.

3. To serve, spoon lentil-rice mixture onto plate. Top with lettuce, tomatoes, cheese and other favorite toppings.

Makes 4½ cups

¾ cup lentil/rice mix provides 0.5 oz. GB and 1.5 oz. MMA. Lettuce and tomato provide ¼ cup VEG for a 3-5 year old at lunch/supper

Snack

Carrot Fries

4 cups carrots, cut into sticks
1 teaspoon cumin
1 teaspoon curry powder
¼ teaspoon salt
¼ teaspoon pepper

1. Preheat oven to 425 degrees. Line a baking sheet with foil and coat with non-stick cooking spray.

2. Coat carrot sticks with the cooking spray and spread them in a single layer on the baking sheet.

3. In a small bowl, stir together the cumin, curry powder, salt and pepper.

4. Sprinkle carrots with the seasonings and bake for 20-25 minutes until tender. Turn over halfway through baking.

Makes 3 cups

½ cup provides ½ cup VEG for a 3-5 year old at snack

Breakfast

Slow Cooker Oatmeal, Milk

	Toddler	Pre-School	School Age
Oatmeal*	1/2 cup	1 cup	1 cup
Milk	1/2 cup	3/4 cup	1 cup

Lunch

Broccoli-Cheese Bites, Whole Grain Crackers, Sugar Snap Peas, Cantaloupe, Milk

	Toddler	Pre-School	School Age
Broccoli-Cheese Bites*	1 bite	2 bites	2 bites
Crackers	3	3	6
Peas	1/8 cup	1/8 cup	1/4 cup
Cantaloupe	1/8 cup	1/4 cup	1/4 cup
Milk	1/2 cup	3/4 cup	1 cup

Snack

Grapes, Whole Grain Crackers

	Toddler	Pre-School	School Age
Grapes	1/2 cup	1/2 cup	3/4 cup
Crackers	3	3	6

Breakfast

Slow Cooker Oatmeal

1 teaspoon butter
6 cups water
3 cups unsweetened applesauce
1¼ cups rolled oats
1½ cups sweet and tart apples,
  cored and diced
1 tablespoon ground cinnamon

1. Lightly grease a 5 quart or larger slow cooker with the butter or cooking spray.

2. In the slow cooker, stir together all the ingredients.

3. Cook on low for 6 hours or overnight.

Makes 4½ cups

 1 cup provides 1 oz. GB and ½ cup FR for a 3-5 year old at breakfast

Lunch

Broccoli-Cheese Bites

3 eggs
⅛ teaspoon black pepper
½ teaspoon Italian seasoning
4 cups frozen broccoli, thawed and chopped
1¾ cups mozzarella cheese, grated
1 cup breadcrumbs

1. Preheat oven to 375 degrees. Line a baking sheet with parchment paper.

2. In a large bowl, beat together the eggs, black pepper and Italian seasoning.

3. Add the broccoli, cheese and breadcrumbs to the eggs and mix well.

4. Hand-form 12 small patties and lay them on the baking sheet.

5. Bake in oven, turning the patties after the first 15 minutes. Bake until golden, about 20-30 minutes total.

Make 12 bites

 2 bites provides 2 oz. MMA and ¼ cup VEG for a 3-5 year old at lunch/supper

SPRING **Week 4** Friday

Breakfast

Super Strata, Blueberries, Milk

	Toddler	Pre-School	School Age
Super Strata*	1/2 strata	1 strata	1 strata
Blueberries	1/4 cup	1/2 cup	1/2 cup
Milk	1/2 cup	3/4 cup	1 cup

Lunch

Mighty Spinach Chicken Quesadillas, Jicama Sticks, Honeydew Drops, Milk

	Toddler	Pre-School	School Age
Quesadillas*	1/4 quesadilla	1/2 quesadilla	1/2 quesadilla
Jicama Sticks	1/8 cup	1/4 cup	1/2 cup
Honeydew Drops	1/8 cup	1/4 cup	1/4 cup
Milk	1/2 cup	3/4 cup	1 cup

Snack

Peanutty Yogurt Dip, Apple Fans

	Toddler	Pre-School	School Age
Dip*	2 tbsp	2 tbsp	4 tbsp
Apple Fans	1/2 cup	1/2 cup	3/4 cup

twist & sprout

Breakfast

Super Strata

3 eggs, beaten
1¼ cups 1% or fat-free milk
½ teaspoon garlic powder
6 slices whole grain bread
4 ounces cooked turkey, chopped small
1 cup broccoli, chopped small
3 ounces cheese, shredded

1. Preheat oven to 350 degrees. Coat an 8 x 8-inch baking dish with cooking spray.

2. In a bowl, beat the eggs and then stir in the milk and garlic powder. Set aside.

3. Tear bread into small pieces. Place ½ of the bread pieces on the bottom of the baking dish. Reserve the other half for topping.

4. Evenly distribute the turkey, broccoli and cheese over the bread. Pour egg mixture over all, followed by the reserved bread pieces.

5. Bake until mixture is firm, about 45 minutes. Let cool slightly and then cut into 6 equal squares.

Makes 6 strata

  1 strata provides 1 oz. GB and 1 oz. MMA for a 3-5 year old at breakfast

Lunch

Mighty Spinach Chicken Quesadillas

2¼ teaspoons butter
1½ cups spinach, chopped
¾ cup tomatoes, chopped
1 cup cooked chicken, chopped
6 small whole wheat tortillas
½ cup salsa
2 cups mozzarella cheese, shredded

1. Preheat oven to 400 degrees. Line a baking sheet with foil and coat with cooking spray.

2. In a large skillet, melt butter over medium heat. Add spinach, tomatoes and chicken. Cook until spinach is wilted, the tomatoes are tender and the chicken is heated through.

3. Place 3 tortillas on the baking sheet. Top each with ⅓ cup of the spinach-chicken mixture, 2 tablespoons salsa and 6 tablespoons cheese. Top each with the reserved tortillas.

4. Bake until the cheese melts, 6 to 8 minutes.

5. To serve, cut in half.

Makes 3 quesadillas

  ½ quesadilla provides 1 oz. GB and 2 oz. MMA for a 3-5 year old at lunch/supper

Snack

Peanutty Yogurt Dip

¼ cup creamy peanut butter
½ cup vanilla low-fat yogurt

1. In a bowl, stir together the peanut butter and yogurt. Refrigerate until ready to serve.

2. Serve with apple fans.

Makes ¾ cup

  2 tablespoons provides 0.5 oz. MMA for a 3-5 year old at snack

Recipe

twist & sprout

Summer Recipes

Breakfast

Happy Flapjacks, Hard Boiled Egg, Strawberries, Milk

	Toddler	Pre-School	School Age
Pancakes*	1/2 pancake	1/2 pancake	1 pancake
Egg	1/2 egg	1/2 egg	1 egg
Strawberries	1/4 cup	1/2 cup	1/2 cup
Milk	1/2 cup	3/4 cup	1 cup

Lunch

Sloppy Sammie on Whole Grain Bun, Peas, Watermelon, Milk

	Toddler	Pre-School	School Age
Sloppy Sammie*	1/3 cup	1/2 cup	2/3 cup
Bun	1/2	1/2	1
Peas	1/8 cup	1/4 cup	1/2 cup
Watermelon	1/8 cup	1/4 cup	1/4 cup
Milk	1/2 cup	3/4 cup	1 cup

Snack

Funky Cabbage Salad, Milk

	Toddler	Pre-School	School Age
Cabbage Salad*	3/4 cup	3/4 cup	1-1/4 cups
Milk	1/2 cup	1/2 cup	1 cup

Breakfast

Happy Flapjacks

1 tablespoon melted butter
1 egg
¾ cup 1% or fat-free milk
½ cup all-purpose enriched flour
½ cup enriched or whole grain cornmeal
1 teaspoon baking powder
½ teaspoon salt
1 teaspoon sugar
½ large Granny Smith apple, cored and diced

1. In a small bowl, beat the butter, egg and milk together with a fork until just blended.

2. In a medium bowl, mix together the flour, cornmeal, baking powder, salt and sugar.

3. Pour the wet ingredients into the bowl of dry ingredients and stir until just moistened. Add the apples and mix until all ingredients are moist.

4. Coat a skillet with non-stick cooking spray and heat over medium heat. Pour ½ cup of the batter onto the skillet for each pancake. Cook until both sides are golden brown.

Makes 8 pancakes

½ pancake provides 0.5 oz. GB
for a 3-5 year old at breakfast

Lunch

Sloppy Sammie

¼ cup onions, chopped
½ cup carrots, grated
¼ cup green peppers, chopped
1 pound ground turkey
½ cup tomato sauce
¾ cup crushed tomatoes
¼ cup barbecue sauce
6 whole wheat hamburger buns

1. Coat skillet with non-stick cooking spray.

2. Add onions, carrots, green pepper and turkey to the pan and sauté over medium-high heat for 5 minutes. Add tomato sauce, crushed tomatoes and barbeque sauce. Bring to a boil.

3. Reduce heat and simmer for 10 minutes, stirring occasionally.

4. Uncover and cook for an additional 3 minutes or until thick.

5. To serve, spoon ½ cup of mixture onto each bun.

Makes 6 sandwiches

1 sandwich provides 1 oz. GB, 1.5 oz. MMA and ¼ cup VEG for a 3-5 year old at lunch/supper

Snack

Funky Cabbage Salad

3 cups green cabbage, shredded
½ cup mandarin oranges, drained
½ cup pineapple, crushed, drained
½ cup mixed berries, thawed
¾ teaspoon honey
3 tablespoons plain low-fat yogurt

1. In a bowl, mix together all ingredients. Refrigerate for an hour before serving.

Makes 4½ cups

¾ cup provides ½ cup VEG
for a 3-5 year old at snack

Breakfast

Sugar & Spice Quesadilla, Milk

	Toddler	Pre-School	School Age
Quesadilla*	1/4 quesadilla	1/2 quesadilla	1/2 quesadilla
Milk	1/2 cup	3/4 cup	1 cup

Lunch

Green Garden Salad, Breadsticks, Apples, Milk

	Toddler	Pre-School	School Age
Salad*	1/2 cup	1 cup	1-1/4 cups
Chicken*	1/4 cup	1/3 cup	1/2 cup
Breadsticks	1/2	1/2	1
Apple Slices	1/8 cup	1/4 cup	1/4 cup
Milk	1/2 cup	3/4 cup	1 cup

Snack

Watermelon Pizza

	Toddler	Pre-School	School Age
Pizza*	1 slice	1 slice	2 slices

Breakfast

Sugar & Spice Quesadillas

3 8-inch whole wheat tortillas
3 tablespoons cream cheese
3 cups sliced strawberries
2 tablespoons sugar
¼ teaspoon ground cinnamon

1. Spread 1 tablespoon cream cheese over each tortilla.

2. Sprinkle one half of each with strawberries, sugar and cinnamon.

3. Fold each tortilla in half.

Makes 3 quesadillas

½ quesadilla provides 1 oz. GB and ½ cup FR for a 3-5 year old at breakfast

Lunch

Green Garden Salad

1 pound boneless, skinless chicken breast
1½ teaspoons dried parsley
1½ teaspoons dried basil
1½ tablespoons olive oil
6 cups mixed salad greens
¾ cup carrots, chopped
¾ cup tomatoes, chopped small
6 tablespoons Italian dressing

1. Preheat oven to 350 degrees. Coat a small baking dish with non-stick spray.

2. In a bowl, toss chicken with olive oil, basil and parsley. Bake for 30 minutes or until internal temperature reaches 165 degrees and juices run clear. Or, coat a skillet with cooking spray and heat pan on medium-high heat. Add marinated chicken and cook 6 minutes on each side or until done.

3. In large bowl, toss greens, carrots, tomatoes.

4. Cut cooked chicken into bite-sized pieces.

5. To serve, place 1 cup of salad mixture on each plate. Top with chicken and 1 tablespoon dressing.

Makes 3 cups chicken, 7½ cups salad mixture

1 cup salad mixture and ⅓ cup chicken provide 1.5 oz. MMA and ½ cup VEG for a 3-5 year old at lunch/supper

Snack

Watermelon Pizza

6 watermelon wedges,
  1-inch thick x 3-inches wide at rind
1½ cups cottage cheese
¾ cup blueberries

1. Top each watermelon slice with ¼ cup cottage cheese and 2 tablespoons blueberries.

Makes 6 watermelon pizzas

1 slice provides 0.5 oz. MMA and ½ cup FR for a 3-5 year old at snack

Breakfast

Parfait Smoothie, Milk

	Toddler	Pre-School	School Age
Smoothie*	1/2 cup	3/4 cup	3/4 cup
Granola Topping*	1/8 cup	1/8 cup	1/4 cup
Milk	1/2 cup	3/4 cup	1 cup

Lunch

Black Bean, Corn & Blueberry Salad, Whole Grain Bread, Grilled Asparagus, Milk

	Toddler	Pre-School	School Age
Salad*	2/3 cup	1 cup	1-1/3 cups
Bread	1/2 slice	1/2 slice	1 slice
Asparagus	1/8 cup	1/8 cup	1/4 cup
Milk	1/2 cup	3/4 cup	1 cup

Snack

Sweet Potato Crisps, Milk

	Toddler	Pre-School	School Age
Crisps*	1/2 cup	1/2 cup	3/4 cup
Milk	1/2 cup	1/2 cup	1 cup

twist & sprout

Breakfast

Parfait Smoothie

2⅓ cups granola, divided
5 cups mixed berries, fresh or frozen
3 cups plain low-fat yogurt

1. Place 1⅓ cup of the granola, all the berries and yogurt in a blender. Blend until smooth.
2. Pour into glasses and sprinkle each smoothie with ⅛ cup granola.

Makes 4½ cups

  ¾ cup smoothie with ⅛ cup granola topping provides 0.5 oz. GB, 1 oz. MMA and ½ cup FR for a 3-5 year old at breakfast

Lunch

Black Bean, Corn & Blueberry Salad

1½ cups blueberries
1½ cups whole kernel corn, thawed or drained
2 15-ounce cans (3 cups) black beans,
   drained and rinsed
3 tablespoons olive oil
1½ teaspoons balsamic vinegar
¾ teaspoon salt
1½ tablespoons lime juice
3 tablespoons cilantro, chopped

1. Place corn in a bowl with the blueberries and beans.
2. In a separate bowl, whisk oil, vinegar, salt, lime juice and cilantro together.
3. Pour dressing over corn and bean mixture and toss to combine.

Makes 6 cups

  1 cup provides 1.5 oz. MMA, ¼ cup VEG and ¼ cup FR for a 3-5 year old at lunch/supper

Snack

Sweet Potato Crisps

5 cups sweet potatoes, thinly sliced
2 tablespoons olive oil
½ teaspoon salt
½ teaspoon paprika

1. Preheat oven to 450 degrees. Line two baking sheets with foil and brush lightly with olive oil.
2. In a large plastic bag or bowl, toss sweet potato with oil and seasonings.
3. Spread sliced potatoes in a single layer on baking sheets.
4. Bake 10 minutes and turn over. Bake until browned and crisp, about 10 more minutes.

Makes 3¾ cups

  ½ cup crisps provides ½ cup VEG for a 3-5 year old at snack

SUMMER Week 1 Thursday

Breakfast

Baked Omelet, Whole Grain Toast, Milk

	Toddler	Pre-School	School Age
Omelet*	1/2 slice	1 slice	1 slice
Toast	1/2 slice	1/2 slice	1 slice
Milk	1/2 cup	3/4 cup	1 cup

Lunch

BBQ Chicken Wraps, Cucumber Slices, Peppy Pineapple, Milk

	Toddler	Pre-School	School Age
Wraps*	1 wrap	2 wraps	2 wraps
Cucumber Slices	1/8 cup	1/8 cup	1/4 cup
Pineapple	1/8 cup	1/4 cup	1/4 cup
Milk	1/2 cup	3/4 cup	1 cup

Snack

Frozen Strawberries with Yogurt

	Toddler	Pre-School	School Age
Strawberries*	1/2 cup	1/2 cup	3/4 cup
Yogurt*	1/4 cup	1/4 cup	1/2 cup

twist & sprout

Breakfast

Baked Omelet

1 teaspoon cooking oil
1¼ cups green bell peppers, chopped
½ cup mushrooms, sliced
6 eggs
1 cup 1% or fat-free milk
½ cup whole wheat flour
1 cup tomatoes, diced
¾ cup salsa
2 ounces cheddar cheese, grated

1. Preheat oven to 450 degrees. Thoroughly grease a 9"x13" baking pan.

2. In a small skillet, heat the oil over medium heat and cook peppers and mushrooms until softened, about 5 minutes.

3. Blend eggs, milk, and flour in a blender until smooth. Add cooked vegetables and tomatoes to the egg mixture, stir well and then pour egg mixture into the baking pan.

4. Bake for 20 minutes. Remove from the oven when the eggs are cooked through.

5. To serve, top with the cheese and salsa. Then, roll up the omelet, starting at the narrow end of the pan. Cut into 6 slices and place on platter.

Makes 6 omelet slices

1 slice provides 1 oz. MMA and ½ cup VEG for a 3-5 year old at breakfast

Lunch

BBQ Chicken Wraps

1 teaspoon olive oil
1¼ pounds boneless, skinless chicken, cut into strips
¼ cup barbeque sauce
½ cup tomatoes, diced
½ cup onions, chopped
1½ cups romaine lettuce, shredded
6 8-inch whole grain tortillas

1. In a large, non-stick skillet heat the oil over medium heat.

2. Add chicken and cook about 6 minutes.

3. Stir in barbeque sauce and simmer over medium heat for 7 to 9 minutes.

4. In a separate bowl, combine tomatoes, onions and lettuce.

5. To assemble, top each tortilla with ½ cup (2 oz.) chicken and ¼ cup of the vegetable mixture. Roll up and cut in half.

Makes 12 wraps

2 wraps provide 1 oz. GB, 2 oz. MMA and ¼ cup VEG for a 3-5 year old at lunch/supper

Snack

Frozen Strawberries with Yogurt

4 cups (1 qt.) strawberries, washed and sliced in half
1½ cups (12 ounces) Greek yogurt, any flavor

1. Slice strawberries in half. Place on baking sheet and freeze for 2 hours.

2. Coat each frozen strawberry half with the yogurt, using a spoon to dip them.

Makes 3 cups

½ cup strawberries and ¼ cup yogurt provides 0.5 oz. MMA and ½ cup FR for a 3-5 year old at snack

Breakfast

Breakfast Banana Splits, Milk

	Toddler	Pre-School	School Age
Banana Splits*	1/2 banana split	1 banana split	1 banana split
Milk	1/2 cup	3/4 cup	1 cup

Lunch

Island Fun Pasta Salad, Cherry Tomatoes, Celery Sticks, Milk

	Toddler	Pre-School	School Age
Salad*	1/2 cup	1 cup	1 cup
Cherry Tomatoes	1/8 cup	1/8 cup	1/4 cup
Celery Sticks	1/8 cup	1/8 cup	1/4 cup
Milk	1/2 cup	3/4 cup	1 cup

Snack

Three Shape Trail Mix, Grapes

	Toddler	Pre-School	School Age
Trail Mix*	3/4 cup	3/4 cup	1-1/4 cups
Grapes	1/2 cup	1/2 cup	3/4 cup

twist & sprout

Breakfast

Breakfast Banana Splits

6 medium bananas
1½ cups (12 ounces) low-fat yogurt, any flavor
2 cups granola, any flavor

1. Cut bananas in half crosswise and then lengthwise.
2. Place 4 pieces of banana in each dish.
3. Top each banana with ¼ cup of yogurt and ¼ cup granola.

Makes 6 banana splits

1 banana split provides 1 oz. GB, 0.5 oz. MMA and ½ cup FR for a 3-5 year old at breakfast

Lunch

Island Fun Pasta Salad

1 cup whole grain spiral pasta, dry
1 teaspoon cooking oil
½ cup plain or vanilla low-fat yogurt
¼ of a fresh orange, juiced
1½ cups spinach, chopped
½ cup peach chunks, drained
¼ cup pineapple chunks, drained
½ cup red cabbage, shredded
¼ cup green onions, chopped
2 15-ounce cans (3 cups) kidney beans,
   drained and rinsed

1. Cook pasta as directed on package. Drain. Toss with the oil to prevent sticking and set aside to cool or chill in refrigerator.
2. In a small bowl, combine the yogurt and juice of the orange to make the dressing.
3. In a large bowl, mix together the pasta, fruits, vegetables and beans.
4. Pour the yogurt dressing over the pasta and mix until well coated.

Makes 6 cups

1 cup provides 1 oz. GB, 2 oz. MMA and ¼ cup VEG for a 3 -5 year old at lunch/supper

Snack

Three Shape Trail Mix

1½ cups "O"-shaped cereal, e.g. Cheerios
1½ cups hexagon-shaped cereal, e.g. Crispix
1½ cups square cereal, e.g. Chex

1. In a bowl, mix all the cereals together.

Makes 4½ cups

¾ cup provides 0.5 oz. GB for a 3-5 year old at snack

SUMMER Week 2 Monday

Breakfast

Sunny Fiesta Wrap, Grapes, Milk

	Toddler	Pre-School	School Age
Fiesta Wrap*	1 wrap	2 wraps	2 wraps
Grapes	1/8 cup	1/4 cup	1/4 cup
Milk	1/2 cup	3/4 cup	1 cup

Lunch

Q Burgers, Shredded Lettuce Salad, Apples, Milk

	Toddler	Pre-School	School Age
Q Burgers*	1/2 burger	1 burger	1 burger
Lettuce Salad*	1/4 cup	1/2 cup	1 cup
Apples	1/8 cup	1/4 cup	1/4 cup
Milk	1/2 cup	3/4 cup	1 cup

Snack

Sweet Strawberry Pudding

	Toddler	Pre-School	School Age
Pudding*	3/4 cup	3/4 cup	1-1/2 cup

70

Breakfast

Sunny Fiesta Wraps

2 teaspoons vegetable oil
1 cup yellow onions, chopped small
1½ 15-ounce cans (2 cups) pinto beans,
   rinsed and drained
1½ tablespoons fresh garlic, minced
1½ teaspoons ground cumin
¼ teaspoon salt
¾ cup salsa
¾ cup cheese, grated
6 8-inch whole wheat tortillas

1. In a large saucepan over medium heat, heat the oil and saute the onions until tender.

2. Add beans, garlic, cumin and salt to the onions and simmer about 10 minutes.

3. Add salsa and cheese and mix well. Remove from heat.

4. To assemble, lay out the tortillas. Spread ½ cup bean mixture down the middle of each tortilla. Roll up, cut in half and serve.

Makes 12 wraps

 2 wraps provide 1 oz. GB and ½ cup VEG
 for a 3-5 year old at breakfast

Lunch

Q Burgers

¾ cup uncooked quinoa
2 15-ounce cans (3 cups) black beans,
   rinsed and drained
⅓ cup carrots, shredded
3 green onions, thinly sliced
3 fresh garlic cloves, minced
⅓ cup breadcrumbs
1 large egg
1½ tablespoons ground cumin
½ tsp salt
¾ teaspoon black pepper
1½ tablespoons olive oil
6 whole wheat hamburger buns
6 ½-ounce slices mozzarella cheese

1. In a saucepan, cook the quinoa according to the package directions. Set aside.

2. If baking, preheat oven to 350 degrees. Coat a baking sheet with non-stick spray.

3. In a large bowl, lightly mash the black beans. Mix in the cooked quinoa and remaining ingredients, except the buns. Form 6 patties.

4. Bake for 30 minutes in oven or coat a skillet with non-stick spray and cook until golden brown and heated through. Top with cheese and heat until melted.

5. To serve, place burgers on buns.

Makes 6 burgers

 1 burger on a bun provides 1 oz. GB and
 2 oz. MMA for a 3-5 year old at lunch/supper

Snack

Sweet Strawberry Pudding

3 cups frozen strawberries or mixed berries,
   thawed and minced
1½ cups (12 oz.) plain Greek-style yogurt
3 tablespoons honey

1. Place all ingredients into bowl and mix.

Makes 4½ cups

 ¾ cup provides 0.5 oz. MMA and ½ cup FR
 for a 3-5 year old at snack

Breakfast

Almond-Raisin Granola, Peaches, Milk

	Toddler	Pre-School	School Age
Granola*	1/4 cup	1/4 cup	1/3 cup
Peaches	1/4 cup	1/2 cup	1/2 cup
Milk	1/2 cup	3/4 cup	1 cup

Lunch

Chinese Pork, Whole Grain Roll, Cabbage Steaks, Carrot Sticks, Milk

	Toddler	Pre-School	School Age
Chinese Pork*	1/4 cup	1/3 cup	1/2 cup
Roll	1/2	1/2	1
Cabbage Steaks*	1/2 steak	1 steak	1 steak
Carrot Sticks	1/8 cup	1/8 cup	1/4 cup
Milk	1/2 cup	3/4 cup	1 cup

Snack

Monkey Milk Shake, Whole Grain Crackers

	Toddler	Pre-School	School Age
Milk Shake*	1 cup	1 cup	1-1/2 cups
Crackers	3	3	6

Breakfast

Almond-Raisin Granola

3 cups regular rolled oats (not instant)
⅔ cup almonds, sliced
⅔ cup sunflower seeds
½ teaspoon ground cinnamon
⅓ cup melted butter
⅓ cup brown sugar
⅛ teaspoon salt
¾ cup raisins

1. Preheat oven to 350 degrees. Line a baking sheet with foil or parchment.

2. In a bowl, mix together all ingredients except raisins. Spread mixture on baking sheet.

3. Bake for 30 minutes or more, stirring occasionally to avoid burning. A longer baking time will yield a crunchier granola.

4. Remove from oven and cool. Once completely cooled, add raisins, and place granola in air-tight container.

Makes about 4½ cups

¼ cup provides 0.5 oz. GB
for a 3-5 year old at breakfast

Lunch

Chinese Pork

1 tablespoon fresh garlic, minced
1 tablespoon fresh ginger, peeled and grated
½ cup green onions, thinly sliced
½ cup soy sauce
½ teaspoon Chinese five spice seasoning
3 tablespoons honey
1 pound boneless pork loin,
    cut into bite-sized pieces

1. In a sturdy, resealable bag, mix together all the seasonings. Add pork and seal the bag.

2. Marinate in the refrigerator for 2 hours or overnight. Turn the bag over several times while marinating to ensure the pork is coated.

3. Preheat oven to 450 degrees. Line a baking sheet with foil and coat with cooking spray.

4. Place pork on baking sheet in a single layer and then on the top rack of the oven.

5. Bake until browned and firm and the internal temperature is 150 degrees, about 20-30 minutes.

Makes 2¾ cups

⅓ cup provides 1.5 oz. MMA
for a 3-5 year old at lunch/supper

Lunch

Cabbage Steaks

½ head green cabbage, about 6-8" in diameter
1 tablespoon olive oil
Salt and pepper

1. Preheat oven to 450 degrees. Coat a baking sheet with non-stick spray.

2. Slice the cabbage into 1-inch thick "steaks." Drizzle with olive oil and sprinkle with salt and pepper.

3. Roast until brown and crispy on top, about 12 minutes.

Makes 6 steaks

1 cabbage steak provides ¼ cup VEG
for a 3-5 year old at lunch/supper

Snack

Monkey Milk Shake

3 cups strawberries, washed, hulled and sliced
3 cups banana chunks
3 cups 1% or skim milk
5 ice cubes

1. Blend in blender until smooth.

Makes 6 cups

1 cup provides ½ cup FR
for a 3-5 year old at snack

SUMMER **Week 2** Wednesday

Breakfast

Oh My Oatmeal, Milk

	Toddler	Pre-School	School Age
Oatmeal*	3/4 cup	3/4 cup	1-1/2 cups
Milk	1/2 cup	3/4 cup	1 cup

Lunch

Baked Meatballs, Blooming Bulgur, Peas, Pineapple, Milk

	Toddler	Pre-School	School Age
Meatballs*	2 meatballs	2 meatballs	3 meatballs
Bulgur*	1/4 cup	1/2 cup	1/2 cup
Peas	1/8 cup	1/8 cup	1/4 cup
Pineapple	1/8 cup	1/4 cup	1/4 cup
Milk	1/2 cup	3/4 cup	1 cup

Snack

Whole Grain Herb Bagel Crisps, Applesauce

	Toddler	Pre-School	School Age
Bagel Crisps*	4 crisps	4 crisps	8 crisps
Applesauce	1/2 cup	1/2 cup	3/4 cup

twist & sprout

Breakfast

Oh My Oatmeal

1½ cups water
¾ cup regular rolled oats
2¼ teaspoons ground cinnamon
3 cups raspberries and blackberries
3 teaspoons honey

1. In a saucepan, combine water, oats, and cinnamon and bring to a boil.
2. Reduce heat and simmer for 5 to 10 minutes or until mixture has thickened.
3. Fold in berries.
4. Drizzle honey over each serving.

Makes 4½ cups

¾ cup provides 0.5 oz. GB and ½ cup FR for a 3-5 year old at breakfast

Recipe for Herb Bagel Crisps on page 77.

Lunch

Baked Meatballs

1 tablespoon vegetable oil
3 tablespoons onion, minced
1 pound lean ground beef (85/15)
1 egg
½ cup breadcrumbs
⅓ cup 1% or fat-free milk
⅛ teaspoon salt
¼ teaspoon pepper
1½ teaspoons onion powder
½ teaspoon garlic powder

1. Preheat oven to 400 degrees. Grease baking sheet lightly with oil.
2. In a small skillet, heat 1 tablespoon of the oil and add onions. Cook over medium heat until tender, about 3 minutes.
3. In a bowl, mix remaining ingredients together. Add cooked onions and mix well.
4. Shape into 12 meatballs and place on baking sheet.
5. Bake until thoroughly cooked, about 10-12 minutes.

Makes 12 meatballs

2 meatballs provide 1.5 oz. MMA for a 3-5 year old at lunch/supper

Lunch

Blooming Bulgur

1 tablespoon canola oil
¾ cup onion, finely chopped
1 cup green bell peppers, finely chopped
1 cup mushrooms, finely chopped
¾ cup bulgur wheat
1½ cups low-sodium chicken broth
½ teaspoon ground cumin
⅓ cup salsa

1. In large skillet, heat oil and add onion, pepper and mushrooms. Cook over medium heat until soft, about 3-5 minutes, stirring occasionally.
2. Add bulgur and cook for 2 minutes, stirring to coat the grain.
3. Add broth, cumin and salsa and bring to a boil. Cover, reduce heat, and simmer slowly for 15 minutes or until the liquid is all absorbed.
4. Remove from heat, let rest for 5 minutes and then serve.

Makes 3 cups

½ cup provides 1 oz. GB and ¼ cup VEG for a 3-5 year old at lunch/supper

Breakfast

Whole Grain Bagel, Nut Butter, Honeydew Drops, Milk

	Toddler	Pre-School	School Age
Bagel	1/2	1/2	1
Nut butter	1 tbsp	1 tbsp	2 tbsp
Honeydew Drops	1/4 cup	1/2 cup	1/2 cup
Milk	1/2 cup	3/4 cup	1 cup

Lunch

Summertime Rice, Roasted Broccoli Trees, Pears, Milk

	Toddler	Pre-School	School Age
Summertime Rice*	2/3 cup	1-1/3 cups	1-3/4 cups
Broccoli Trees	1/8 cup	1/4 cup	1/4 cup
Pears	1/8 cup	1/4 cup	1/4 cup
Milk	1/2 cup	3/4 cup	1 cup

Snack

Cool as a Cucumber Dip, Carrot Sticks

	Toddler	Pre-School	School Age
Cucumber Dip*	1/3 cup	1/3 cup	2/3 cup
Carrot Sticks	1/2 cup	1/2 cup	3/4 cup

Snack Week 2, Wednesday

Herb Bagel Crisps

3 1-ounce whole grain bagels
1 tablespoon melted butter
2 tablespoons olive oil
2 cloves fresh garlic, minced
1 teaspoon dried basil

1. Preheat oven to 325 degrees.

2. Cut each bagel into 8 ¼-inch slices.

3. Stir together the olive oil, butter and garlic. Brush oil on one side of each bagel slice. Sprinkle with basil.

4. Place on ungreased baking sheet and bake until crisp, about 10-12 minutes.

Makes 24 crisps

4 crisps provide 0.5 oz. GB
for a 3-5 year old at snack

Lunch

Summertime Rice

1 cup brown rice
¾ cup tomatoes, chopped
3 cups spinach, chopped
¾ cup carrots, chopped
¾ cup broccoli, chopped
2 15-ounce cans (3 cups) chickpeas,
   rinsed and drained
2 tablespoons olive oil
2 tablespoons apple cider vinegar
1½ tablespoons Parmesan cheese, grated

1. Cook rice according to package instructions. Set aside to cool.

2. In a bowl, mix together all the vegetables, except the beans.

3. In a separate bowl, mix together the cooled rice and the chickpeas.

4. Add the vegetables to the rice and bean mixture.

5. In a small bowl, mix together the olive oil and vinegar. Pour over rice and chickpeas; stir to coat.

6. Top with Parmesan cheese and stir to mix.

Makes 6 cups

1⅓ cups provide 1 oz. GB, 1.5 oz. MMA and
½ cup VEG for a 3-5 year old at lunch/supper

Snack

Cool as a Cucumber Dip

1½ tablespoons olive oil
½ teaspoon fresh garlic, finely minced
⅛ teaspoon salt
⅛ teaspoon black pepper
1½ cups plain low-fat yogurt
¾ cup cucumbers, peeled, seeded
   and finely chopped
⅛ teaspoon dried dill
3 cups carrot sticks

1. In a bowl, stir well the olive oil, garlic, salt, pepper and yogurt.

2. Add the cucumber and dill and stir well.

3. Chill one hour before serving, if possible.

Makes 2 cups dip

⅓ cup dip and ½ cup carrot sticks provides
0.5 oz. MMA and ½ cup VEG for a 3-5 year
old at snack

Breakfast

Scrambled Eggs, Toast, Blueberries, Milk

	Toddler	Pre-School	School Age
Eggs	1/4 cup	1/4 cup	1/2 cup
Toast	1/2 slice	1/2 slice	1 slice
Blueberries	1/4 cup	1/2 cup	1/2 cup
Milk	1/2 cup	3/4 cup	1 cup

Lunch

Fun Fish Nuggets, Citrus Couscous, Corn and Peas, Orange Wedges, Milk

	Toddler	Pre-School	School Age
Fish Nuggets*	2 nuggets	3 nuggets	4 nuggets
Citrus Couscous*	1/4 cup	1/4 cup	1/2 cup
Corn & Peas	1/8 cup	1/4 cup	1/2 cup
Orange Wedges	1/8 cup	1/4 cup	1/4 cup
Milk	1/2 cup	3/4 cup	1 cup

Snack

Bold Black Bean Dip, Sugar Snap Peas

	Toddler	Pre-School	School Age
Bean Dip*	2 tbsp	2 tbsp	4 tbsp
Snap Peas	1/2 cup	1/2 cup	3/4 cup

twist & sprout

Lunch

Fun Fish Nuggets

½ cup breadcrumbs
⅛ teaspoon pepper
⅛ teaspoon paprika
¼ teaspoon dried parsley, rubbed
3 tablespoons Parmesan cheese, finely grated
2 eggs, beaten
1 pound tilapia, cut into 18 bite-sized pieces

1. Pre-heat oven at 400 degrees. Line a baking sheet with foil and coat with non-stick spray.

2. In a plastic bag, mix the breadcrumbs , pepper, paprika, dried parsley and cheese.

3. Dip the fish pieces into the eggs and place in the bag of breadcrumbs . Seal and shake the bag to coat all sides. Put the fish chunks in the bag and shake to coat all sides.

4. Bake until lightly golden and firm to the touch, about 12-15 minutes.

Makes 18 nuggets

3 nuggets provide 1.5 oz. MMA
for a 3-5 year old at lunch/supper

Lunch

Citrus Couscous

¾ teaspoon orange zest
¾ cup water
2½ teaspoons olive oil or butter
¼ teaspoon salt
3 tablespoons fresh orange juice
¾ cup couscous, dry
¾ of a green onion, thinly sliced

1. Wash orange thoroughly. Using a zester, remove zest of orange and set aside.

2. In a medium saucepan, combine water, olive oil or butter and salt. Bring to a boil and add the orange juice.

3. Remove saucepan from the heat, add couscous and stir until thoroughly mixed. Cover the pan and let stand for 5-7 minutes.

4. Fluff the couscous with a fork until separated and then stir in the reserved orange zest. Cover until ready to serve.

5. To serve, fluff the couscous again and sprinkle the green onion on top.

Makes 1½ cups

¼ cup provides 0.5 oz. GB
for a 3-5 year old at lunch/supper

Snack

Bold Black Bean Dip

½ 15-ounce can (¾ cup) black beans, rinsed and drained
2 tablespoons red bell peppers, chopped small
½ teaspoon ground cumin
1½ tablespoons lime juice
1 tablespoon olive oil
½ teaspoon fresh garlic, chopped
3 cups sugar snap peas

1. Combine all ingredients, except the snap peas, in food processor and process until smooth, about 1-2 minutes.

2. Serve with whole sugar snap peas.

Makes ¾ cup

2 tablespoons dip and ½ cup sugar snap peas provide 0.5 oz. MMA and ½ cup VEG for a 3-5 year old at snack

Breakfast

Crunchy Fruit Kabobs, Milk

	Toddler	Pre-School	School Age
Fruit Kabobs*	1 kabob	2 kabobs	2 kabobs
Milk	1/2 cup	3/4 cup	1 cup

Lunch

Golden Spiced Chicken, Whole Grain Roll, Spinach and Radish Wheel Salad, Watermelon Bites, Milk

	Toddler	Pre-School	School Age
Chicken*	1/2 piece	1 piece	1 piece
Roll	1/2	1/2	1
Spinach Salad	1/4 cup	1/2 cup	1 cup
Watermelon Bites	1/8 cup	1/4 cup	1/4 cup
Milk	1/2 cup	3/4 cup	1 cup

Snack

Gooey Towers

	Toddler	Pre-School	School Age
Gooey Towers*	2 towers	2 towers	4 towers

SUMMER Week 3 Monday

Breakfast

Crunchy Fruit Kabobs

1 cup canned chunk pineapple, drained
1 cup cantaloupe, cubed
1 cup honeydew melon, cubed
½ cup grapes
3 large strawberries
¾ cup vanilla low-fat yogurt
1½ cups granola

1. Thread fruit on skinny cocktail straws or long toothpicks.
2. Place yogurt and granola in separate shallow bowls or plates.
3. Roll each kabob in the yogurt and then in the granola.

Makes 12 kabobs

 2 kabobs provide 1 oz. GB and ½ cup FR
 for a 3-5 year old at breakfast

Lunch

Golden Spiced Chicken

1 teaspoon olive oil
1¼ pounds boneless, skinless chicken breast
½ teaspoon garlic powder
½ teaspoon ground cinnamon
½ teaspoon curry powder
½ teaspoon ground cloves
1 cup low-sodium chicken broth
1½ cups apple juice
½ cup raisins

1. In a large skillet, heat oil over medium heat. Add chicken and cook until just browned on both sides, about 2 minutes per side.
2. In a small bowl, stir together the garlic powder, cinnamon, curry powder and cloves. Sprinkle over the chicken.
3. Add broth, apple juice and raisins to the skillet and stir. When the liquid starts to simmer, reduce heat to medium-low. Cook chicken, stirring occasionally, until firm, about 5 minutes.
4. To serve, place chicken on plate and drizzle with the pan juices. Cut into 6 pieces.

Makes 6 pieces

 1 piece provides 2 oz. MMA
 for a 3-5 year old at lunch/supper

Snack

Gooey Towers

¾ cup peanut/nut butter
1½ cups celery, chopped
12 whole grain crackers (similar to Triscuits)
6 tablespoons raisins

1. In a bowl, stir the celery and nut butter until well mixed.
2. To assemble, lay crackers in a row. Place about 2 tablespoons of the nut butter mixture on each cracker and top with ½ tablespoon of raisins.

Makes 12 towers

 2 towers provide 0.5 oz. GB and 0.5 oz. MMA
 for a 3-5 year old at snack

Breakfast

Pancake Smiles, Berries, Milk

	Toddler	Pre-School	School Age
Pancakes*	1 pancake	1 pancakes	2 pancakes
Berries	1/4 cup	1/2 cup	1/2 cup
Milk	1/2 cup	3/4 cup	1 cup

Lunch

Turkey Apple Takers, Broccoli Trees, Citrus Corn, Milk

	Toddler	Pre-School	School Age
Turkey Takers*	1/2 sandwich	1 sandwich	1 sandwich
Broccoli Trees	1/8 cup	1/4 cup	1/2 cup
Citrus Corn*	1/8 cup	1/4 cup	1/4 cup
Milk	1/2 cup	3/4 cup	1 cup

Snack

Peachy Smoothie

	Toddler	Pre-School	School Age
Peachy Smoothie*	3/4 cup	3/4 cup	1-1/4 cups

twist & sprout

82

Breakfast

Pancake Smiles

1½ cups whole wheat flour
2 teaspoons baking powder
¼ teaspoon salt
2 eggs
1½ cups 1% or fat-free milk
2 tablespoons butter
1½ cups fresh strawberries, sliced
1½ cups blueberries

1. In a bowl, combine flour, baking powder, salt.

2. In separate bowl, whisk eggs and milk until just mixed.

3. Add wet mixture to the dry ingredients, stirring gently. Batter will be thick.

4. Coat large skillet with non-stick cooking spray and then heat over medium heat.

5. Pour ⅓ cup of the batter onto the skillet for each pancake. Cook on both sides until golden brown.

6. To serve, outline pancakes with the strawberries and make two eyes and a smile with the blueberries.

Makes 12 pancakes

1 pancake with ½ cup berries provides 0.5 oz. GB and ½ cup FR for a 3-5 year old at breakfast

Lunch

Turkey Apple Takers

3 tablespoons Dijon mustard
3 tablespoons honey
1½ tablespoons butter
6 slices whole wheat bread
6 1-ounce slices Swiss cheese
¾ cup Granny Smith apples, thinly sliced
6 ounces turkey breast, thinly sliced

1. Spread waxed paper or plastic wrap on work surface.

2. In a small bowl, stir together the mustard and honey.

3. Spread butter on the top side of each slice of bread. Flip the bread over and spread mustard on the other side. Set aside three of the bread slices.

4. On the remaining bread slices, stack two slices of cheese, the apple slices and the turkey. Top the turkey with the reserved bread slices, mustard side down, buttered side up.

5. Heat a large nonstick skillet over medium-high heat. Add sandwiches to pan and cook until bread is browned and cheese melts, about 2 minutes on each side. To serve, cut in half.

Makes 6 sandwich halves

1 sandwich provides 2 oz. GB and 2 oz. MMA for a 3-5 year old at lunch/supper

Lunch

Citrus Corn

3 cups frozen whole kernel corn, thawed
3 tablespoons butter
1½ teaspoons lime zest
Salt to taste

1. In saucepan, melt the butter. Add the corn and cook over medium heat for 1-2 minutes.

2. Sprinkle corn with lime zest and salt and stir. Cook an additional 5 minutes.

Makes 3 cups

¼ cup provides ¼ cup VEG for a 3-5 year old at lunch/supper

Snack

Peach Smoothie

1½ cups (12 oz.) yogurt, any flavor
3 cups frozen peaches

1. In a food processor, blend yogurt and peaches.

2. Pour mixture into six 8-ounce cups.

Makes 4½ cups smoothie

¾ cup provides 2 oz. MMA and ½ cup FR for a 3-5 year old at snack

SUMMER **Week 3** Wednesday

Breakfast

Fruity Quinoa, Milk

	Toddler	Pre-School	School Age
Quinoa*	1/2 cup	1 cup	1 cup
Milk	1/2 cup	3/4 cup	1 cup

Lunch

Sweet Swirl Wrap, Celery Sticks, Grapes, Milk

	Toddler	Pre-School	School Age
Swirl Wrap*	1 wrap	2 wraps	2 wraps
Celery sticks	1/8 cup	1/4 cup	1/2 cup
Grapes	1/8 cup	1/4 cup	1/4 cup
Milk	1/2 cup	3/4 cup	1 cup

Snack

Cucumber Canoes, Milk

	Toddler	Pre-School	School Age
Cucumber Canoes*	2 canoes	2 canoes	4 canoes
Milk	1/2 cup	1/2 cup	1 cup

Breakfast

Fruity Quinoa

1½ cups water
¾ cup dry quinoa
⅛ teaspoon salt
¾ teaspoon brown sugar
1½ cups raspberries
1½ cups of pears, diced

1. In medium saucepan, bring water and quinoa to a boil. Add salt and brown sugar. Cover and reduce heat to a simmer. Simmer until water is absorbed and quinoa is tender, about 12-15 minutes.

2. When quinoa is cooked, remove from heat and fold in fruit.

Makes 6 cups

1 cup provides 1 oz. GB and ½ cup FR for a 3-5 year old at breakfast

Lunch

Sweet Swirl Wrap

6 8-inch whole grain tortillas
6 ounces low-sodium deli ham, thinly sliced
6 ounces cheddar cheese, sliced
6 tablespoons honey mustard dressing
½ cup carrots, shredded
6 tablespoons raisins

1. To assemble, lay tortillas on work surface. Top with ham and then cheese.

2. Drizzle ham and cheese with honey mustard.

3. Sprinkle with shredded carrot and raisins.

4. Roll each tortilla tightly. Cut in half, keeping open side down on plate so it doesn't unroll.

Makes 12 wraps

2 wraps provide 1 oz. GB, 2 oz. MMA for a 3-5 year old at lunch/supper

Snack

Cucumber Canoes

1½ large cucumbers
6 ounces cottage cheese
6 baby carrots, cut in half lengthwise

1. Cut cucumbers in half lengthwise and scoop out the seeds.

2. Fill the "canoe" with the cottage cheese. Lay baby carrots on top for the "paddles."

3. Cut both cucumber halves into 4 pieces, crosswise and the half cucumbers into 2 pieces.

Makes 12 mini canoes

2 mini canoes provide 0.5 oz. MMA and ½ cup VEG for a 3-5 year old at snack

Breakfast

Eggs in a Nest, Apple Bites, Milk

	Toddler	Pre-School	School Age
Eggs in a Nest*	1/2 nest	1 nest	1 nest
Apple Bites	1/4 cup	1/2 cup	1/2 cup
Milk	1/2 cup	3/4 cup	1 cup

Lunch

Roast Pork with Red Pepper Sauce, Savory Brown Rice, Mighty Minty Peas, Banana Wheels, Milk

	Toddler	Pre-School	School Age
Pork*	2 pieces	3 pieces	4 pieces
Rice	1/4 cup	1/4 cup	1/2 cup
Minty Peas*	1/8 cup	1/4 cup	1/2 cup
Bananas	1/8 cup	1/4 cup	1/4 cup
Milk	1/2 cup	3/4 cup	1 cup

Snack

Go Fish Snack, Carrot Sticks

	Toddler	Pre-School	School Age
Nut Butter*	1 tbsp	1 tbsp	2 tbsp
Goldfish Crackers*	1/4 cup	1/4 cup	1/2 cup
Pretzel Rod*	1/2	1	1
Carrot Sticks	1/2 cup	1/2 cup	3/4 cup

Breakfast

Eggs in a Nest

6 slices whole grain bread
6 eggs

1. Toast bread and cut a small circle out of the center with the top of a small drinking glass.
2. Lightly spray one side of the toast with non-stick cooking spray.
3. Heat skillet over medium-high heat. Place toast, coated side down, in skillet. Crack one egg directly into the cut-out circle of each slice.
4. Cover skillet and cook until eggs are completely cooked. Top egg with the circle of bread.

Makes 6 nests

1 nest provides 1 oz. GB and 2 oz. MMA for a
3-5 year old at breakfast

Lunch

Roast Pork with Red Pepper Sauce

3½ cups red bell peppers, chopped
½ cup low-sodium chicken broth
1 tablespoon apple cider vinegar
2 tablespoons tomato paste
2 teaspoons dried leaf oregano
2 teaspoons garlic powder
1 teaspoon honey
¼ teaspoon ground black pepper
¼ teaspoon salt
1¼ pounds boneless pork loin,
    cut into 20 bite-sized pieces

1. In blender, combine all ingredients except pork and blend until smooth.
2. In large plastic bag, combine sauce with pork, and marinate for at least 2 hours or overnight.
3. Pre-heat oven to 400 degrees F.
4. Line a shallow pan with foil. Lay pork and sauce on pan and place on top rack.
5. Cook pork in oven until browned and firm, about 25-30 minutes and internal temperature is 150 degrees.

Makes 20 pieces

3 pieces provides 1.5 oz. MMA
for a 3-5 year old at lunch/supper

Lunch

Mighty Minty Peas

3 cups sweet peas, frozen
3 tablespoons butter
3 teaspoons fresh mint, chopped or ¼ tsp dried
¼ teaspoon salt

1. In small skillet, melt butter over medium heat. Add peas, cover and cook until bright in color, about 2-3 minutes, stirring frequently.
2. Sprinkle chopped mint and salt over peas. Stir and cook until peas are hot, about 1 minute.

Makes 3 cups

¼ cup provides ¼ cup VEG
for a 3-5 year old at lunch/supper

Snack

Go Fish Snack

6 tablespoons peanut/nut butter
6 large pretzel rods
1½ cups goldfish crackers

1. Place nut butter, one pretzel rod and goldfish crackers on individual plates.
2. Let the kids dip their pretzel rods into the nut butter and "fish" for the goldfish crackers.

Makes 6 snacks

¼ cup crackers, 1 pretzel rod and 1 tbsp nut butter provide 1 oz. GB and 0.5 oz. MMA for a 3-5 year old at snack

SUMMER Week 3 Friday

Breakfast

Cinnamon Berry Treasures, Milk

	Toddler	Pre-School	School Age
Treasures*	1	2	2
Milk	1/2 cup	3/4 cup	1 cup

Lunch

Captain's Zesty Chicken, Power Penne, Peach Smiles, Milk

	Toddler	Pre-School	School Age
Chicken*	1/4 cup	1/3 cup	1/2 cup
Power Penne*	3/4 cup	3/4 cup	1-1/2 cups
Peach Smiles	1/8 cup	1/4 cup	1/4 cup
Milk	1/2 cup	3/4 cup	1 cup

Snack

Pineapple-Cottage Cheese Yummies

	Toddler	Pre-School	School Age
Pineapple Rings*	3	3	5
Cottage Cheese*	1/4 cup	1/4 cup	1/2 cup

Breakfast

Cinnamon Berry Treasures

1½ tablespoons melted butter
6 8-inch whole grain tortillas
½ teaspoon ground cinnamon
3 teaspoons sugar
1½ cups low-fat yogurt, any flavor
3 cups berries, any kind
3 teaspoons honey

1. Preheat oven to 400 degrees. Line a baking sheet with foil or parchment paper. Brush lightly with melted butter.

2. Cut each tortilla in half. Arrange tortilla halves in single layer on the baking sheet.

3. In a small bowl, combine the cinnamon and sugar. Sprinkle tortillas with cinnamon sugar.

4. Bake until crisp and slightly browned, about 4 minutes. Remove from oven.

5. Spread 2 tablespoons yogurt and sprinkle ¼ cup berries onto each tortilla half. Drizzle each with ½ teaspoon honey and fold in half. Yogurt will soften the tortillas enough to fold.

Makes 12 treasures

2 treasures provide 1 oz. GB, 0.5 oz. MMA and ½ cup FR for a 3-5 year old at breakfast

Lunch

Captain's Zesty Chicken

1 teaspoon olive oil
1 cup salsa
1 tablespoon brown sugar
1 teaspoon Dijon mustard
1 pound boneless, skinless chicken breast, cut into bite-sized pieces

1. Preheat the oven to 375 degrees. Coat a shallow baking pan with the olive oil.

2. In a medium bowl, stir together the salsa, brown sugar and mustard. Mix in the chicken.

3. Place seasoned chicken in the baking pan and cover with foil.

4. Bake for 25 minutes. Remove foil, stir and bake uncovered until chicken is firm to the touch, about 15 minutes.

Makes 3 cups

⅓ cup chicken provides 1.5 oz. MMA for a 3-5 year old at lunch/supper

Recipe for Pineapple-Cottage Cheese Yummies is found on page 100.

Lunch

Power Penne

1 cup whole grain penne pasta
1 cup low-sodium chicken broth
1 15-ounce can (1½ cups) black beans, rinsed and drained
2 ounces cold cream cheese, cubed
1 pound frozen spinach, thawed and drained
1 cup cherry tomatoes, halved

1. Cook pasta per package instructions.

2. While pasta is cooking, heat large skillet over medium heat. Add broth and black beans and simmer until heated through, about 3 minutes.

3. Stir in cream cheese and spinach. Return to a simmer, stirring occasionally, about 5 minutes.

4. Add cherry tomatoes and cook until they are warmed through, about 2 minutes.

5. In a large bowl, mix pasta and vegetable sauce.

Makes about 5 cups

¾ cup provides 0.5 oz. GB and ½ cup VEG for a 3-5 year old at lunch/supper

Breakfast

Bananas Foster Parfait, Milk

	Toddler	Pre-School	School Age
Parfait*	1/2 parfait	1 parfait	1 parfait
Milk	1/2 cup	3/4 cup	1 cup

Lunch

Italian Flag Pasta, Awesome Asapargus, Grapes, Milk

	Toddler	Pre-School	School Age
Pasta*	1-1/4 cups	1-1/4 cups	2-2/3 cups
Awesome Asaparagus*	1 spear	2 spears	2 spears
Grapes	1/8 cup	1/4 cup	1/4 cup
Milk	1/2 cup	3/4 cup	1 cup

Snack

Green Pepper Posies, Milk

	Toddler	Pre-School	School Age
Posies*	1 posie	1 posie	2 posies
Milk	1/2 cup	1/2 cup	1 cup

Breakfast

Bananas Foster Parfait

6 medium ripe bananas
1½ tablespoons brown sugar
1½ tablespoons apple juice
3 tablespoons butter
1½ cups low-fat yogurt, any flavor
1½ cups granola, any type

1. Peel bananas. Cut each in half lengthwise and then crosswise.

2. In a nonstick skillet, melt the butter over medium-low heat. Stir in brown sugar and apple juice. Cook until mixture begins to bubble, about 3 minutes.

3. Add bananas to pan, flat sides down, and cook until bananas begin to soften, about 2 minutes.

4. To assemble, place 4 slices of banana into each bowl or cup. Top with ¼ cup yogurt and 1/4 cup granola.

Makes 6 parfaits

1 parfait provides 1 oz. GB, 0.5 oz. MMA and ½ cup FR for a 3-5 year old at breakfast

Lunch

Italian Flag Pasta

1 cup whole grain spiral pasta, dry
½ teaspoon oil
¼ cup pesto
3 cups cooked chicken
2 cups cherry tomatoes, quartered
Parmesan cheese, shredded, for garnish

1. Cook pasta per package instructions. Drain and cover to stay warm.

2. In large skillet, heat oil over medium heat. Add pesto and chicken and cook until warmed through.

3. Add cooked pasta. Heat until pasta is warmed through. Remove from heat. Mix in tomatoes.

4. To serve, garnish with Parmesan cheese.

Makes 7 cups

1¼ cups provides 0.5 oz. GB, 1.5 oz. MMA and ¼ cup VEG for a 3-5 year old at lunch/supper

Recipe for Awesome Asparagus is found on page 100.

Snack

Green Pepper Posies

12 cherry tomatoes
2 green peppers

1. Cut cherry tomatoes in half.

2. Cut the ends off each pepper. Thinly slice the ends into strips for leaves.

3. Cut the middle of each pepper into three wide rings.

4. Arrange green pepper rings and strips as the flower blossom and stem.

5. Arrange the tomato slices as leaves.

Makes 6 posies

1 posie provides ½ cup VEG for a 3-5 year old at snack

Breakfast

Little Boy Blue Muffins, Blueberries, Milk

	Toddler	Pre-School	School Age
Muffin*	1/2 muffin	1/2 muffin	1 muffin
Blueberries	1/4 cup	1/2 cup	1/2 cup
Milk	1/2 cup	3/4 cup	1 cup

Lunch

Summertime Tuna Bites, Broccoli Slaw, Peas, Milk

	Toddler	Pre-School	School Age
Tuna Bites*	2 bites	3 bites	6 bites
Broccoli Slaw	1/8 cup	1/4 cup	1/2 cup
Peas	1/8 cup	1/4 cup	1/4 cup
Milk	1/2 cup	3/4 cup	1 cup

Snack

Crunchy Rosemary Chickpeas, Milk

	Toddler	Pre-School	School Age
Chickpeas*	1/2 cup	1/2 cup	3/4 cup
Milk	1/2 cup	1/2 cup	1 cup

Breakfast

Little Boy Blue Muffins

½ cup regular rolled oats
1 cup 1% or fat-free milk
1½ cups whole wheat flour
1 tablespoon baking powder
¼ teaspoon salt
1 egg, lightly beaten
⅓ cup brown sugar
¼ cup canola oil
½ cup blueberries
½ cup blackberries

1. Preheat the oven to 400 degrees. Line two 12-cup muffin pans with paper liners.

2. In a bowl, stir together the oats and milk. Microwave 3 minutes.

3. In a large bowl, whisk together the flour, baking powder and salt.

4. In another small bowl, beat the egg, then mix in the brown sugar and canola oil.

5. Add both the oatmeal and the egg mixture to the flour. Mix just until moistened but still slightly lumpy. Gently fold in the blueberries and blackberries.

6. Spoon batter into the muffin cups, filling each ⅔ full. Bake until the tops are golden brown, about 15-18 minutes.

Makes 14 muffins

 ½ muffin provides 0.5 oz. GB
 for a 3-5 year old at breakfast

Lunch

Summertime Tuna Bites

3 5-ounce cans water-packed albacore tuna, drained and flaked
¼ cup cheese, shredded
2 tablespoons cream cheese, softened
2 tablespoons mayonnaise
¾ cup pineapple tidbits, drained
1 tablespoon almonds, chopped
18 whole wheat crackers (e.g. Triscuits)

1. In a bowl, combine tuna, cheese, cream cheese and mayonnaise, mixing well. Chill until ready to serve.

2. Before serving, stir the pineapple and almonds into the tuna spread.

3. Spread 2½ tablespoons tuna filling onto each cracker.

Makes 18 tuna bites

 3 tuna bites provide 0.5 oz. GB and 1.5 oz MMA for a 3-5 year old at lunch/supper

Snack

Rosemary Crunchy Chickpeas

1 15-ounce can (1½ cups) chickpeas, rinsed and drained
1½ tablespoons olive oil
¾ teaspoon garlic powder
1 tablespoon fresh rosemary, minced
¼ teaspoon lemon juice
¼ teaspoon salt

1. Preheat oven to 375 degrees. Line a baking sheet with foil or parchment. Coat with non-stick cooking spray.

2. In a small bowl, stir together the oil and seasonings. Add the chickpeas and toss until well coated.

3. Place chickpeas on the baking sheet and bake until golden and crispy, about 30-40 minutes.

Makes 1½ cups

 ½ cup of chickpeas provides ½ cup VEG
 for a 3-5 year old at snack

Breakfast

Rise and Shine Cereal, Milk

	Toddler	Pre-School	School Age
Cereal*	1/2 cup	1 cup	1 cup
Milk	1/2 cup	3/4 cup	1 cup

Lunch

Picnic Pinwheels, Cucumber Spears, Watermelon, Milk

	Toddler	Pre-School	School Age
Pinwheel Sandwiches*	2 pinwheels	4 pinwheels	4 pinwheels
Cucumber Spears	1/8 cup	1/8 cup	1/4 cup
Watermelon	1/8 cup	1/4 cup	1/4 cup
Milk	1/2 cup	3/4 cup	1 cup

Snack

Mr. Tomato Head

	Toddler	Pre-School	School Age
Stuffed Tomato*	1 tomato	1 tomato	2 tomatoes

Breakfast

Rise & Shine Cereal

2 cups water
¼ teaspoon salt
⅓ cup whole grain farina
1½ cups peaches, chopped
1½ cups blueberries, chopped

1. In a saucepan, bring water and salt to a boil.

2. Slowly add the farina, stirring constantly with whisk until well blended.

3. Return to a boil. Reduce heat to low and simmer, uncovered, 2½ minutes or until thickened, stirring frequently.

4. Reserve a few berries and peaches for garnish. Fold the remaining fruit into the cooked farina.

5. To serve, garnish each serving with the berries and peaches.

Makes 6 cups

1 cup provides 1 oz. GB and ½ cup FR for a 3-5 year old at breakfast

Lunch

Picnic Pinwheels

6 8-inch whole wheat flour tortillas
½ cup low-sodium marinara sauce
6 cups fresh spinach, washed, dried, chopped
3 cups (12 oz.) mozzarella cheese, shredded

1. Preheat oven to 450 degrees. Line a baking sheet with foil and coat with non-stick spray.

2. Place tortillas on the baking sheet and spread 1 tablespoon marinara sauce over each.

3. Sprinkle 1 cup spinach over each tortilla and then ½ cup cheese.

4. Place baking sheet on the top oven rack and bake until cheese melts, about 1 to 2 minutes. Remove from oven.

5. Immediately roll up the tortilla. Allow to cool for a few minutes before slicing into 4 pinwheels/roll-ups.

6. To serve, place 4 pieces side by side on each plate, cut sides up to show colors.

Makes 24 pinwheels

4 pinwheels provides 1 oz. GB, 2 oz MMA and ½ cup VEG for a 3-5 year old at lunch/supper

Snack

Mr. Tomato Head

6 medium tomatoes
¾ cup couscous, uncooked
3 cups low-sodium vegetable broth
⅓ cup fresh basil, julienned
12 black olive slices
2 slices provolone cheese

1. Slice the top off each tomato and reserve for "hat." Hollow out each tomato, chop pulp and reserve.

2. In a saucepan, bring vegetable broth to a boil. Stir in couscous, remove from heat, cover and set aside to cool for 5-7 minutes.

3. Add reserved pulp to cooked couscous and fill tomato with cooked couscous mix, top with the basil for "hair" and cover partially with reserved tomato top.

4. Place the black olive slices on the outside of the tomato for eyes.

5. Cut 6 smiles out of provolone cheese and place them below the "eyes."

Makes 6 stuffed tomatoes

1 stuffed tomato provides 0.5 oz. GB and ½ cup VEG for a 3-5 year old at snack

Breakfast

Farmers Pizza, Grapes, Milk

	Toddler	Pre-School	School Age
Pizza*	1/2 pizza	1/2 pizza	1 pizza
Grapes	1/4 cup	1/2 cup	1/2 cup
Milk	1/2 cup	3/4 cup	1 cup

Lunch

Colorful Roll-Up, Whole Grain Roll, Cantaloupe Moons, Milk

	Toddler	Pre-School	School Age
Roll-Up Sandwich*	1/2 roll-up	1 roll-up	1 roll-up
Roll	1/2	1/2	1
Cantaloupe Moons	1/8 cup	1/4 cup	1/4 cup
Milk	1/2 cup	3/4 cup	1 cup

Snack

Sunflower Snacks

	Toddler	Pre-School	School Age
Cheese*	0.5 oz.	0.5 oz.	1 oz.
Grapes*	1/2 cup	1/2 cup	3/4 cup

twist & sprout

96

Breakfast

Farmers Pizza

3 whole wheat English muffins, split
3 teaspoons butter
6 large tomato slices
3 hard boiled eggs, sliced
6 tablespoons mozzarella cheese, shredded
½ teaspoon dried leaf oregano, crumbled
½ teaspoon kosher salt

1. Preheat broiler. Line a baking sheet with foil.

2. Toast English muffins under the broiler. Butter each half and place on baking sheet.

3. Top each muffin with a tomato slice, egg slices (½ an egg per serving) and 1 tablespoon cheese. Sprinkle oregano and kosher salt over all.

4. Broil until cheese melts, about 5 minutes.

Makes 6 pizzas

  1 pizza provides 1 oz. GB and 1 oz. MMA
  for a 3-5 year old at breakfast

Lunch

Colorful Roll-Ups

6 ounces low-sodium deli turkey, sliced
¾ cup hummus
6 ½-ounce slices Swiss cheese
12 6-inch celery sticks
1½ cups red bell peppers, cut into strips

1. Lay out 6 1-ounce slices of turkey and spread 2 tablespoons hummus on each. Top each with one slice of cheese.

2. Place 2 celery sticks and ¼ cup red pepper strips at top end of the turkey slice and roll up.

Makes 6 roll-ups

  1 roll-up provides 2 oz. MMA and ½ cup VEG
  for a 3-5 year old at lunch/supper

Snack

Sunflower Snacks

6 ounces cheddar cheese, sliced
3 cups grapes

1. Cut cheddar cheese into triangles and arrange in a circle with the points out to form a sunflower.

2. Fill center of "sunflower" with grapes

Makes 6 sunflowers

  0.5 oz. cheese and ½ cup grapes
  provide 0.5 oz. MMA and ½ cup FR
  for a 3-5 year old at snack

Breakfast

Toasted O's Cereal, Strawberries, Milk

	Toddler	Pre-School	School Age
Cereal	1/2 cup	1/2 cup	1 cup
Strawberries	1/4 cup	1/2 cup	1/2 cup
Milk	1/2 cup	3/4 cup	1 cup

Lunch

Pockets of Gold, Roasted Parmesan Potatoes, Peaches, Milk

	Toddler	Pre-School	School Age
Pocket Sandwich*	1 pocket	1 pocket	2 pockets
Parmesan Potatoes*	1/8 cup	1/4 cup	1/2 cup
Peaches	1/8 cup	1/4 cup	1/4 cup
Milk	1/2 cup	3/4 cup	1 cup

Snack

Ants on a Raft, Milk

	Toddler	Pre-School	School Age
Ants on a Raft*	3 rafts	3 rafts	5 rafts
Milk	1/2 cup	1/2 cup	1 cup

twist & sprout

98

Lunch

Pockets of Gold

3 whole wheat pita rounds
6 hard boiled eggs, peeled and chopped
3 tablespoons mayonnaise
¾ teaspoon mustard
⅓ cup carrots, shredded
1½ tablespoons green onion, sliced thin
3 cups romaine lettuce, shredded

1. Cut pita rounds in half, then slice open the pockets and toast.

2. In a bowl, place chopped eggs, mayonnaise, mustard, carrots and green onion. Stir until well combined.

3. Spread a heaping ¼ cup egg salad inside each toasted pita pocket and stuff with ½ cup lettuce greens.

Makes 6 pita pockets

1 pocket provides 0.5 oz. GB and 1.5 oz. MMA for a 3-5 year old at lunch/supper

Lunch

Roasted Parmesan Potatoes

1½ pounds potatoes, diced
2 tablespoons olive oil
⅛ teaspoon salt
⅛ teaspoon pepper
⅓ cup Parmesan cheese, grated
1 teaspoon dried parsley

1. Preheat oven to 375 degrees. Line baking sheet with parchment paper.

2. In a bowl, toss potatoes with the olive oil, salt and pepper.

3. Place potatoes in a single layer on baking sheet.

4. Bake until lightly golden, crispy on the outside and soft on the inside, about 25 to 35 minutes.

5. Remove from oven, place in bowl and toss with the Parmesan cheese and parsley.

Makes about 3¼ cups

¼ cup provides ¼ cup VEG for 3-5 year old at lunch/supper

Snack

Ants on a Raft

3 cups bananas, peeled and sliced
   into 18 wheels
½ cup peanut or nut butter
3 tablespoons raisins

1. Lay banana slices on a plate. Place about 1 teaspoon nut butter on each slice.

2. Top each raft with raisins.

Makes 18 rafts

3 rafts provide 0.5 oz. MMA and ½ cup FR for a 3-5 year old at snack

Recipes

Lunch

Awesome Asparagus

12 asparagus spears, woody ends removed
  (about 1¼ pounds)
2 tablespoons olive oil
¼ teaspoon salt
¼ teaspoon pepper

1. Preheat oven to 400 degrees. Coat a small baking pan with non-stick spray.

2. In the pan, coat the asparagus with the olive oil and season with the salt and pepper.

3. Roast until bright green and tender, with a slight crunch, from 5 to 10 minutes.

Makes 12 asparagus spears

  2 spears provide ¼ cup VEG
  for a 3-5 year old at lunch/supper

*This recipe is on the lunch menu for
Summer, Week 4, Monday.
See page 90.*

Snack

Pineapple-Cottage Cheese Yummies

18 pineapple rings, drained
  (about 2-20 oz. cans)
1½ cups cottage cheese

1. Pat pineapple rings dry. Reserve 12 rings.

2. Place 6 pineapple rings on individual plates. Scoop ⅛ cup cottage cheese into the center of each ring. Top each with a second pineapple ring to make a "sandwich."

3. Scoop another ⅛ cup cottage cheese into the center of the second ring and top with another pineapple ring to make a double-decker "sandwich."

Makes 6 ring sandwiches

  1 ring sandwich provides 0.5 oz. MMA and
  ¼ cup FR for a 3-5 year old at snack

*This recipe is the snack on
Summer, Week 3, Friday.
See page 88.*

twist & sprout Autumn Recipes

..Tasty!

AUTUMN Week 1 Monday

Breakfast

Fiesta Egg Puff, Whole Grain Toast, Milk

	Toddler	Pre-School	School Age
Fiesta Egg Puff*	1/2 puff	1 puff	1 puff
Toast	1/2 slice	1/2 slice	1 slice
Milk	1/2 cup	3/4 cup	1 cup

Lunch

Beany Power Pita Sandwich, Carrot and Celery Sticks, Applesauce, Milk

	Toddler	Pre-School	School Age
Pita Sandwich*	1 pocket	1 pocket	2 pockets
Carrot & Celery Sticks	1/8 cup	1/8 cup	1/4 cup
Applesauce	1/8 cup	1/4 cup	1/4 cup
Milk	1/2 cup	3/4 cup	1 cup

Snack

Cauliflower Popcorn, Milk

	Toddler	Pre-School	School Age
Cauliflower Popcorn*	1/2 cup	1/2 cup	3/4 cup
Milk	1/2 cup	1/2 cup	1 cup

twist & sprout

Breakfast

Fiesta Egg Puff

1 tablespoon unsalted butter
1 cup mushrooms, sliced
½ cup tomatoes, diced
4 cups spinach, loosely packed
1 cup red bell peppers, seeded and diced
6 eggs
1½ cups potatoes, cooked and grated
½ cup mozzarella cheese, shredded

1. Preheat oven to 400 degrees. Line large muffin tin with 6 greased foil cupcake liners.

2. Heat butter in large skillet over medium-high heat. Add mushrooms, tomatoes, spinach and peppers. Cook for 5 minutes or until tender and water has evaporated. Remove from heat and set aside to cool.

3. In large bowl, lightly beat eggs. Mix in cooked vegetables, potatoes and cheese. Season with salt and pepper.

4. Divide egg mixture evenly into liners.

5. Bake in oven for 10-20 minutes or until eggs are puffy and firm.

Makes 6 puffs

1 puff provides 2 oz. MMA and ½ cup VEG for a 3-5 year old at breakfast

Lunch

Beany Power Pita Sandwich

1 15-ounce can (1½ cups) black beans, rinsed and drained
¾ cup cherry tomatoes, chopped
½ cup salsa
½ cup guacamole
3 whole wheat pita rounds
6 romaine lettuce leaves
1 cup cheddar cheese, shredded

1. In a medium bowl, mix black beans, cherry tomatoes, salsa and guacamole.

2. Cut each pita round in half, then slice open the pockets.

3. Stuff each pocket with lettuce and black bean mixture. Sprinkle with cheese.

Makes 6 pocket sandwiches

1 pocket sandwich provides 1 oz. GB, 1.5 oz. MMA and ¼ cup VEG for a 3-5 year old at lunch/supper

Snack

Cauliflower Popcorn

1 head cauliflower, cut into florets
4 tablespoons olive oil
1 teaspoon salt
½ teaspoon turmeric

1. Preheat oven to 425 degrees. Line a baking sheet with foil or parchment paper.

2. Trim the cauliflower and cut into small, even-sized florets.

3. In a large bowl, toss cauliflower with oil and spices.

4. Spread cauliflower evenly on a lined baking sheet. Roast about 20 minutes or until cauliflower is browned and crunchy.

Makes 3 cups

½ cup provides ½ cup VEG for a 3-5 year old at snack

Breakfast

Banana Rama Breakfast, Milk

	Toddler	Pre-School	School Age
Toast*	1/2 slice	1/2 slice	1 slice
Cottage Cheese*	1/8 cup	1/8 cup	1/4 cup
Bananas*	1/2 banana	1 banana	1 banana
Milk	1/2 cup	3/4 cup	1 cup

Lunch

Olé Chicken Tostada, Roasted Broccoli & Cauliflower Crowns, Pear Rings, Milk

	Toddler	Pre-School	School Age
Tostada*	1/4 tostada	1/2 tostada	1/2 tostada
Broccoli & Cauliflower*	1/8 cup	1/4 cup	1/2 cup
Pear Rings	1/8 cup	1/4 cup	1/4 cup
Milk	1/2 cup	3/4 cup	1 cup

Snack

Whole Grain Crackers, Apple Slices

	Toddler	Pre-School	School Age
Crackers	3	3	6
Apple Slices	1/2 cup	1/2 cup	3/4 cup

twist & sprout

Breakfast

Banana Rama Breakfast

3 slices whole wheat bread, toasted
1½ cups cottage cheese
6 medium bananas, sliced
1½ teaspoons ground cinnamon

1. Toast bread.

2. Spoon cottage cheese onto toast. Arrange sliced bananas on top of cottage cheese and sprinkle with cinnamon.

3. Cut each slice in half and serve.

Makes 6 half slices

1 half slice provides 0.5 oz. GB, 1 oz. MMA and ½ cup FR for a 3-5 year old at breakfast

Lunch

Olé Chicken Tostada

½ pound cooked chicken, shredded, sliced or diced
1 tablespoon salsa
3 8-inch whole wheat tortillas
1 cup cheddar cheese, shredded

1. Preheat oven to 350 degrees.

2. Mix chicken with salsa; set aside.

3. Lay tortillas on a sheet pan. On each tortilla, spread ¼ cup cheese and then 2 ounces chicken; leave unrolled.

4. Bake for about 5-8 minutes or until cheese is melted and very lightly browned.

6. Remove from oven and roll up.

Makes 3 tostadas

½ tostada provides 1 oz. GB and 2 oz. MMA for a 3-5 year old at lunch/supper

Snack

Roasted Broccoli & Cauliflower Crowns

2½ cups cauliflower, cut into florets
2½ cups broccoli, cut into florets
½ teaspoon salt
1 tablespoon olive oil

1. Preheat oven to 425 degrees. Line a baking sheet with foil or parchment paper.

2. Trim the cauliflower and broccoli into small, even-sized florets.

3. In a large bowl, toss cauliflower and broccoli with the oil and salt.

4. Spread evenly on a lined baking sheet and roast until browned and crunchy, about 20 minutes.

Makes 4 cups

¼ cup provides ¼ cup VEG for a 3-5 year old at lunch/supper

Breakfast

Apple Snapple Oatmeal, Milk

	Toddler	Pre-School	School Age
Oatmeal*	3/4 cup	3/4 cup	1-1/2 cups
Milk	1/2 cup	3/4 cup	1 cup

Lunch

English Muffin Vegetable Pizza, Lovely Little Peas, Peaches, Milk

	Toddler	Pre-School	School Age
English Muffin Pizza*	1/2 pizza	1 pizza	1 pizza
Peas	1/8 cup	1/8 cup	1/4 cup
Peaches	1/8 cup	1/4 cup	1/4 cup
Milk	1/2 cup	3/4 cup	1 cup

Snack

Carrots and Hummus Dip

	Toddler	Pre-School	School Age
Carrots	1/2 cup	1/2 cup	3/4 cup
Hummus*	2 tbsp	2 tbsp	1/4 cup

Breakfast

Apple Snapple Oatmeal

1 medium apple or pear, diced
3 cups 100% apple juice
¾ cup regular oatmeal (not instant)
¼ cup raisins
¼ teaspoon ground cinnamon

1. In saucepan, mix together chopped apple or pear, apple juice, oatmeal, raisins and cinnamon.
2. Cook over medium-high heat until bubbly. Then turn burner to low and simmer for 5 minutes, stirring occasionally.

Makes 4½ cups

¾ cup provides 0.5 oz. GB and ½ cup FR for a 3-5 year old at breakfast

Lunch

English Muffin Vegetable Pizza

3 whole wheat English muffins, split
¾ cup low-sodium marinara sauce
¼ cup green peppers, diced
¼ cup mushrooms, diced
¼ cup olives, sliced
¼ cup tomatoes, diced
12 ounces (3 cups) cheese, shredded

1. Preheat oven to 350 degrees.
2. Split English muffins into 6 rounds and toast.
3. Spread each toasted muffin with marinara sauce and then top with vegetables and cheese.
4. Bake in oven until heated through and cheese is melted, about 10 minutes.

Makes 6 pizzas

1 pizza provides 1 oz. GB, 2 oz. MMA and ¼ cup VEG for a 3-5 year old at lunch/supper

Snack

Hummus

1 15-ounce can (1½ cups) chickpeas
½ teaspoon ground cumin
2 tablespoons lemon juice
3 cloves fresh garlic, minced

1. Place all ingredients in a food processor and process until smooth.

Makes ¾ cup

2 tablespoons provides 0.5 oz. MMA for a 3-5 year old at snack

Breakfast

Oatmeal-Carrot Muffin, Banana, Milk

	Toddler	Pre-School	School Age
Muffin*	1/2 muffin	1/2 muffin	1 muffin
Banana	1/2	1	1
Milk	1/2 cup	3/4 cup	1 cup

Lunch

Scrumptious Chicken Drumsticks, Whole Grain Roll, Green Beans, Pineapple, Milk

	Toddler	Pre-School	School Age
Drumsticks*	1	1	2
Roll	1/2 roll	1/2 roll	1 roll
Green Beans	1/8 cup	1/4 cup	1/2 cup
Pineapple	1/8 cup	1/4 cup	1/4 cup
Milk	1/2 cup	3/4 cup	1 cup

Snack

Cinnamon Toast, Warm-You-Up Cider

	Toddler	Pre-School	School Age
Cinnamon Toast	1/2 slice	1/2 slice	1 slice
Cider*	1/2 cup	1/2 cup	3/4 cup

Breakfast

Oatmeal-Carrot Muffins

1 cup whole wheat flour
½ teaspoon baking soda
½ teaspoon salt
2 teaspoons baking powder
½ teaspoon ground cinnamon
1 cup 1% or fat-free milk
1 egg, beaten
½ cup brown sugar, packed
¼ cup melted butter
1 cup quick cooking oats
1 cup carrots, grated

1. Preheat oven to 375 degrees. Line a 12-cup muffin pan with paper baking cups.

2. In a bowl, mix together the flour, baking soda, salt, baking powder and cinnamon.

3. In a separate bowl, whisk together the milk, egg, sugar and butter.

4. Add the wet ingredients to the dry ingredients. Add oats and carrots and mix well.

5. Spoon mixture into the muffin cups, about ⅔ full.

6. Bake for 25 minutes.

Makes 12 muffins

½ muffin provides 0.5 oz. GB
for a 3-5 year old at breakfast

Lunch

Scrumptious Chicken Drumsticks

6 chicken drumsticks
¼ teaspoon paprika
1 teaspoon dried leaf oregano
½ teaspoon coarsely ground black pepper
1 teaspoon dried leaf thyme
¼ teaspoon garlic powder
2 tablespoons lemon juice
1 tablespoon honey or sugar (optional)

1. Wash chicken and pat dry.

2. In large bowl, combine spices with the lemon juice (and honey) to make the seasoning.

3. Rub seasoning over chicken, cover and marinate in refrigerator for at least 5 hours or overnight.

4. Preheat oven to 350 degrees. Line a baking sheet with foil or parchment paper.

5. Place chicken on lined baking sheet and bake, uncovered, until golden brown, about 30 minutes.

6. Turn chicken over and bake until second side is golden brown and the internal temperature is 166 degrees, about 30 minutes.

Makes 6 drumsticks

1 drumstick provides 1.5 oz. MMA
for a 3-5 year old at lunch/supper

Snack

Warm-You-Up Cider

3 cups 100% apple juice or apple cider
¾ cup 100% cranberry juice
1 teaspoon ground cinnamon
½ teaspoon nutmeg
½ orange, thinly sliced

1. In saucepan, combine all ingredients and simmer.

2. Remove from heat and cool slightly before serving.

Makes 3¾ cups

½ cup provides ½ cup FR
for a 3-5 year old at snack

AUTUMN Week 1 Friday

Breakfast

Hocus Pocus Griddlecakes, Scrambled Eggs, Applesauce, Milk

	Toddler	Pre-School	School Age
Pancakes*	1/2	1	1
Scrambled Eggs	1/4 cup	1/4 cup	1/2 cup
Applesauce	1/4 cup	1/2 cup	1/2 cup
Milk	1/2 cup	3/4 cup	1 cup

Lunch

Lavish Lasagna, Spinach Salad, Orange Smiles, Milk

	Toddler	Pre-School	School Age
Lasagna*	1 cup	1 cup	1-3/4 cups
Spinach Salad	1/8 cup	1/8 cup	1/4 cup
Orange Smiles	1/8 cup	1/4 cup	1/4 cup
Milk	1/2 cup	3/4 cup	1 cup

Snack

Peaches, Yogurt

	Toddler	Pre-School	School Age
Peaches	1/2 cup	1/2 cup	3/4 cup
Yogurt	1/4 cup	1/4 cup	1/2 cup

Breakfast

Hocus Pocus Griddlecakes

½ cup whole wheat flour
½ cup quick oatmeal
1 tablespoon sugar
1¼ teaspoons baking powder
¼ teaspoon salt
½ cup 1% or fat-free milk
1 egg
1 tablespoon butter
½ teaspoon ground cinnamon
⅛ teaspoon ground ginger
1 tablespoon honey
Dash nutmeg

1. Preheat a lightly oiled griddle or frying pan over medium-high heat.

2. Place all ingredients in a blender or food processor and puree until smooth.

3. Pour the batter onto the griddle, about ¼ cup for each pancake.

4. Brown on both sides and serve.

Makes 6 pancakes

1 pancake provides 1 oz. GB
for a 3-5 year old at breakfast

Lunch

Lavish Lasagna

2 tablespoons olive oil
2 cups mushrooms, chopped
1 cup green bell peppers, seeded and chopped
1 cup yellow onions, finely chopped
3 cups loosely packed spinach, chopped
16 ounces 2% cottage cheese
3 cups mozzarella cheese, shredded and divided
¼ teaspoon salt
1 26-ounce jar low-sodium pasta sauce
2 large zucchini, sliced into ¼-inch thick rounds
8 ounces no-boil lasagna noodles

1. Heat oil in large skillet over medium heat. Add mushrooms, peppers, onions and spinach. Sauté 5 minutes or until water evaporates.

2. Reserve ½ cup mozzerella cheese. In bowl, combine the cottage cheese, the remaining 2½ cups mozzarella cheese and salt.

3. Coat slow cooker with non-stick cooking spray.

4. Layer ingredients in the slow cooker, as follows: cover bottom with ⅓ of pasta sauce and top with half of the noodles, cooked vegetables, zucchini and cottage cheese.

5. Follow with another ⅓ of the pasta sauce and the remaining half of the noodles, vegetables, zucchini and cottage cheese.

6. Top with remaining pasta sauce. Sprinkle reserved mozzarella cheese on top.

7. Cook on low for 5 hours or until noodles and zucchini are tender.

Makes about 12 cups

1 cup provides 0.5 oz. GB, 1.5 oz. MMA and ½ cup VEG for a 3-5 year old at lunch/supper

Breakfast

Veggie Pancakes, Orange Smiles, Milk

	Toddler	Pre-School	School Age
Veggie Pancakes*	1 pancake	2 pancakes	2 pancakes
Orange Smiles	1/8 cup	1/4 cup	1/4 cup
Milk	1/2 cup	3/4 cup	1 cup

Lunch

Oven Sloppy Joes on Whole Grain Buns, Spunky Spinach, Crazy Crinkle Carrots, Milk

	Toddler	Pre-School	School Age
Sloppy Joes*	1/4 cup	1/3 cup	1/2 cup
Bun	1/2 bun	1/2 bun	1 bun
Spunky Spinach*	1/8 cup	1/4 cup	1/2 cup
Carrots	1/8 cup	1/4 cup	1/4 cup
Milk	1/2 cup	3/4 cup	1 cup

Snack

Apple Boats, Milk

	Toddler	Pre-School	School Age
Apple Boats	1/2 cup	1/2 cup	3/4 cup
Milk	1/2 cup	1/2 cup	1 cup

twist & sprout

Breakfast

Veggie Pancakes

1½ cups zucchini, finely grated
¾ cup carrots, grated
¾ cup whole kernel corn, thawed or drained
1 egg, beaten
1½ tablespoons plain low-fat yogurt
¼ teaspoon salt
⅛ teaspoon pepper
½ cup whole wheat flour
½ cup enriched or whole grain yellow cornmeal
1 teaspoon baking powder
⅓ cup cheddar cheese, grated
1½ tablespoons vegetable oil

1. In a large bowl, combine the zucchini, carrots and corn. Stir in the egg, yogurt, salt and pepper.

2. In a small bowl, whisk together the flour, cornmeal and baking powder. Add flour mixture to the vegetables. Sprinkle cheese over the vegetables and mix well.

3. In a large skillet, heat oil over medium heat. Pour batter into the heated skillet. Flatten with a fork while cooking. Turn over and brown the second side.

Makes 12 pancakes

2 pancakes provide 1 oz. GB and
¼ cup VEG for a 3-5 year old at breakfast

Lunch

Oven Sloppy Joes

1 pound lean ground beef (85/15)
7½ ounces tomato sauce
2 tablespoons ketchup
2 teaspoons brown sugar
¾ cup onions, chopped
⅛ teaspoon Tabasco or hot sauce
½ teaspoon mustard
½ teaspoon vinegar
½ teaspoon Worcestershire sauce
¼ teaspoon pepper

1. Preheat oven to 350 degrees. Coat a small roasting pan with non-stick cooking spray.

2. In a small bowl, mix the tomato sauce, ketchup, brown sugar, onions and spices.

3. Place uncooked hamburger in the roasting pan. Pour sauce mixture over it and mix well. (It is not necessary to brown the hamburger first.)

4. Bake for 1 hour, stirring occasionally.

Makes 2 cups

⅓ cup provides 1.5 oz. MMA and ⅛ cup VEG for a 3-5 year old at lunch/supper

Lunch

Spunky Spinach

¼ cup tomato sauce
½ teaspoon Italian seasoning
1 pound frozen spinach,
   thawed, water squeezed out
1¾ cups kidney beans, rinsed and drained
⅛ teaspoon salt
⅛ teaspoon black pepper

1. In saucepan over medium heat, mix together tomato sauce and Italian seasoning.

2. Add spinach, beans, salt and pepper.

3. Simmer for 10 minutes.

Makes 3 cups

¼ cup provides ¼ cup VEG for a 3-5 year old at lunch/supper

Breakfast

Super Fruity Salsa, Whole Grain Toast, Milk

	Toddler	Pre-School	School Age
Salsa*	1/4 cup	1/2 cup	1/2 cup
Toast	1/2 slice	1/2 slice	1 slice
Milk	1/2 cup	3/4 cup	1 cup

Lunch

Little Bo Peep Pot Pie, Jicama Sticks, Watermelon, Milk

	Toddler	Pre-School	School Age
Pot Pie*	1 slice	1 slice	1-1/2 slices
Jicama	1/8 cup	1/4 cup	1/4 cup
Watermelon	1/8 cup	1/4 cup	1/4 cup
Milk	1/2 cup	3/4 cup	1 cup

Snack

Roasted Chickpeas, Milk

	Toddler	Pre-School	School Age
Chickpeas*	1/2 cup	1/2 cup	3/4 cup
Milk	1/2 cup	1/2 cup	1 cup

twist & sprout

Breakfast

Super Fruity Salsa

3 cups pineapple, drained and diced
3 cups apples, diced
1½ pears, diced

1. In a bowl, mix together all ingredients.

Makes 4½ cups

½ cup provides ½ cup FR
for a 3-5 year old at breakfast

Lunch

Little Bo Peep Pot Pie

Filling

¼ cup onions, chopped
1 tablespoon vegetable oil
1 10-ounce package spinach,
   thawed and water squeezed out
1 cup frozen mixed vegetables
2 tablespoons enriched flour
1 14-ounce can low-sodium chicken broth
1¼ cups potatoes, chopped
¼ cup cheddar cheese, shredded
2½ cups cooked chicken, diced
¼ teaspoon garlic powder

Lunch

Crust

1 cup whole wheat flour
4 tablespoons very cold butter

1. Preheat oven to 350 degrees.

2. In large skillet over medium heat, sauté onions in oil for 5-8 minutes.

3. Add the spinach and mixed vegetables and cook for 5 minutes. Add flour and broth and bring to a boil, simmer until thickened. Add potatoes, cheese, chicken and garlic powder.

4. Pour mixture into a 9-inch pie plate.

5. In a bowl, cut the butter into the flour. On a floured surface, roll out the crust.

6. Place crust over the pie filling, turning the edges under and cutting several slits in top.

7. Bake for 45 minutes or until crust is golden brown.

Makes 8 slices

1 slice provides 1 oz. GB, 1.5 oz. MMA
and ¼ cup VEG for a 3-5 year old
at lunch/supper

Snack

Roasted Chickpeas

3 15-ounce cans (4½ cups) chickpeas,
   rinsed and drained
3 tablespoons olive oil
1½ teaspoons ground cumin
1½ teaspoons chili powder
¾ teaspoon cayenne pepper
¾ teaspoon sea salt

1. Preheat oven to 400 degrees with rack in top section of oven. Coat a baking sheet with non-stick cooking spray.

2. In a large bowl, toss the chickpeas with the oil and spices until evenly coated.

3. Spread the chickpeas in an even layer on the baking sheet. Bake until crisp, about 30 to 40 minutes.

Makes 5 cups

½ cup provides ½ cup VEG
for a 3-5 year old at snack

AUTUMN Week 2 Wednesday

Breakfast

Whole Grain Toast, Scrambled Eggs, Banana, Milk

	Toddler	Pre-School	School Age
Scrambled Eggs	1/4 cup	1/4 cup	1/2 cup
Toast	1/2 slice	1/2 slice	1 slice
Banana	1/2	1/2	1
Milk	1/2 cup	3/4 cup	1 cup

Lunch

Long Live Lemon Chicken, Whole Grain Roll, Tiny Tasty Edamame, Mandarin Oranges, Milk

	Toddler	Pre-School	School Age
Chicken*	1 piece	1 piece	1-1/2 piece
Roll	1/2 roll	1/2 roll	1 roll
Edamame	1/8 cup	1/4 cup	1/2 cup
Mandarin Oranges	1/8 cup	1/4 cup	1/4 cup
Milk	1/2 cup	3/4 cup	1 cup

Snack

Big League Black Bean Salsa, Whole Grain Tortilla Chips

	Toddler	Pre-School	School Age
Black Bean Salsa*	1/2 cup	1/2 cup	3/4 cup
Tortilla Chips	5	5	10

118

Lunch

Long Live Lemon Chicken

¾ cup cherry tomatoes, halved
2 teaspoons Italian seasoning
3 tablespoons Parmesan cheese, grated
1½ tablespoons lemon juice
2 teaspoons olive oil
12 ounces boneless, skinless chicken breasts,
   cut into 6 2-ounce portions

1. Preheat oven to 350 degrees. Line a baking dish with foil or parchment paper, or coat with cooking spray.

2. In a large bowl, toss cherry tomatoes with the Italian seasoning, parmesan cheese, lemon juice and olive oil.

3. Add chicken and stir to coat with marinade. Cover and marinate for 10-15 minutes.

4. Lay chicken in a single layer in the baking dish. Bake until lightly golden and firm to the touch, about 30 minutes.

Makes 6 pieces

 1 piece provides 1.5 oz. MMA
 for a 3-5 year old at lunch/supper

Snack

Big League Black Bean Salsa

1½ 15-ounce cans (2 cups) black beans,
   rinsed and drained
1½ cups tomatoes, chopped
⅓ cup onions, chopped
⅓ cup green bell peppers, chopped
1½ tablespoons lime juice
½ teaspoon cumin
½ teaspoon chili powder
Salt, to taste

1. In large bowl, mix beans and vegetables.

2. Add lime juice and spices. Mix thoroughly.

Makes 3 cups

 ½ cup provides ½ cup VEG
 for a 3-5 year old at snack

AUTUMN Week 2 Thursday

Breakfast

Hungry Bunny Muffin, String Cheese, Grapes, Milk

	Toddler	Pre-School	School Age
Muffin*	1/2 muffin	1/2 muffin	1 muffin
String Cheese	1/2 piece	1/2 piece	1 piece
Grapes	1/4 cup	1/2 cup	1/2 cup
Milk	1/2 cup	3/4 cup	1 cup

Lunch

Rainbow Turkey Wrap, Cheery Cherry Tomatoes, Apple Rings, Milk

	Toddler	Pre-School	School Age
Turkey Wrap*	1/2 wrap	1 wrap	1 wrap
Tomatoes	1/4 cup	1/2 cup	1/2 cup
Apple Rings	1/8 cup	1/4 cup	1/4 cup
Milk	1/2 cup	3/4 cup	1 cup

Snack

Pumpkin Pie Dip, Mini Pretzels

	Toddler	Pre-School	School Age
Pumpkin Pie Dip	1/3 cup	1/3 cup	2/3 cup
Mini Pretzels	9	9	17

twist & sprout

Breakfast

Hungry Bunny Muffins

1 cup whole wheat flour
¼ cup brown sugar
1½ teaspoons baking powder
½ teaspoon ground cinnamon
2 eggs, beaten
½ cup applesauce
2 tablespoons canola or vegetable oil
1 tablespoon lemon juice
½ cup carrots, finely grated

1. Preheat oven to 375 degrees. Line a 6-cup muffin pan with greased foil cupcake liners.

2. In a large bowl, mix together the dry ingredients.

3. In separate bowl, beat together the eggs, applesauce, oil and lemon juice. Stir in the carrots.

3. Make a well in the center of the dry ingredients and add the wet ingredients. Stir just until moistened then spoon into cupcake liners.

4. Bake for 20-25 minutes.

Makes 6 muffins

½ muffin provides 0.5 oz. GB
for a 3-5 year old at breakfast

Lunch

Rainbow Turkey Wraps

6 8-inch whole wheat tortillas
6 teaspoons light ranch dressing
12 ounces low-sodium turkey, sliced
6 ½-ounce slices of cheese
1 large tomato, sliced
1 cup carrots, shredded
½ cup whole kernel corn, thawed or drained
½ cup cucumbers, thinly sliced
1 avocado, peeled and thinly sliced
1 cup purple cabbage, shredded

1. Lay tortillas on cutting board. Spread each tortilla with 1 teaspoon of dressing.

2. Place 2 ounces of turkey and ½ ounce of cheese on each tortilla.

3. Top cheese with the tomatoes, carrots, corn, cucumbers, avocado and cabbage.

4. Roll up the tortillas and serve.

Makes 6 wraps

1 wrap provides 1 oz. GB, 2 oz. MMA and
½ cup VEG for a 3-5 year old at lunch/supper

Snack

Pumpkin Pie Dip

1 cup vanilla low-fat yogurt
1 cup canned pumpkin
1 tablespoon ground cinnamon
⅛ teaspoon ground cloves
⅛ teaspoon ground allspice
⅛ teaspoon ground nutmeg
2 tablespoons brown sugar

1. In a small bowl, mix together all ingredients.

Makes 2 cups

⅓ cup provides 0.5 oz. MMA
for a 3-5 year old at snack

Breakfast

Gorgeous Granola, Blueberries, Milk

	Toddler	Pre-School	School Age
Granola*	1/8 cup	1/8 cup	1/4 cup
Blueberries	1/4 cup	1/2 cup	1/2 cup
Milk	1/2 cup	3/4 cup	1 cup

Lunch

Sweet Salmon, Brown Rice, Sugar Snap Peas, Red Pepper Slices, Milk

	Toddler	Pre-School	School Age
Salmon*	1 filet	1 filet	1-1/2 filets
Brown Rice	1/4 cup	1/4 cup	1/2 cup
Snap Peas	1/8 cup	1/4 cup	1/2 cup
Red Pepper Slices	1/8 cup	1/4 cup	1/4 cup
Milk	1/2 cup	3/4 cup	1 cup

Snack

Clementine Pumpkins, Yogurt, Raspberries

	Toddler	Pre-School	School Age
Clementines*	1	1	2
Yogurt	1/4 cup	1/4 cup	1/2 cup
Raspberries	1/8 cup	1/8 cup	1/4 cup

Breakfast

Gorgeous Granola

5 cups rolled oats (regular, not instant)
1¼ cups coconut, shredded
1 teaspoon ground cinnamon
¼ teaspoon ground ginger
½ cup butter, melted
½ cup brown sugar
¼ teaspoon salt

1. Preheat oven to 350 degrees. Line a baking sheet with foil or parchment paper.

2. In large bowl, combine all ingredients.

3. Spread mixture on baking sheet.

4. Bake for 30 minutes or longer, stirring occasionally. A longer baking time will result in a crunchier granola. Do not burn.

5. Remove from oven and cool baking sheet on a cooling rack.

6. Once completely cooled, place granola in airtight container. It will keep for months.

Makes 6 cups

⅛ cup provides 0.5 oz. GB
for a 3-5 year old at breakfast

Lunch

Sweet Salmon

6 2-ounce salmon filets
2 tablespoons honey
2 tablespoons olive oil
½ teaspoon lemon juice

1. Preheat oven to 375 degrees with a rack in the middle. Line a baking sheet with foil or parchment paper.

2. In a small bowl, mix honey, olive oil and lemon juice. Set aside.

3. Place salmon filets on lined baking sheet. Spoon honey mixture over salmon filets.

4. Bake until fish is firm, about 7-10 minutes.

Makes 6 filets

1 filet provides 1.5 oz. MMA
for a 3-5 year old at lunch/supper

Snack

Clementine Pumpkins

6 clementines
6 celery sticks

1. Peel clementines. Insert celery stick into the center of each clementine to make a "stem."

Makes 6 pumpkins

1 pumpkin provides ⅜ cup FR
for a 3-5 year old at snack

Breakfast

Peachy Parfait, Milk

	Toddler	Pre-School	School Age
Yogurt*	1/4 cup	1/4 cup	1/2 cup
Peaches*	1/4 cup	1/2 cup	1/2 cup
Granola*	1/8 cup	1/8 cup	1/4 cup
Milk	1/2 cup	3/4 cup	1 cup

Lunch

Tropical Turkey Meatloaf, Whole Grain Roll, Green Beans, Clever Cauliflower, Milk

	Toddler	Pre-School	School Age
Meatloaf*	1/2 slice	3/4 slice	1 slice
Roll	1/2	1/2	1
Green Beans	1/8 cup	1/4 cup	1/2 cup
Cauliflower	1/8 cup	1/4 cup	1/4 cup
Milk	1/2 cup	3/4 cup	1 cup

Snack

Apples, Yogurt

	Toddler	Pre-School	School Age
Apple	1/2 cup	1/2 cup	3/4 cup
Yogurt	1/4 cup	1/4 cup	1/2 cup

Breakfast

Peachy Parfait

3 cups peaches, drained, chopped
3 cups plain low-fat yogurt
1½ cups granola

1. Spoon ½ cup fruit into the glass for a bottom layer.
2. Spread ¼ cup yogurt on top of fruit.
3. Layer ⅛ cup granola on top of yogurt.

Makes 6 parfaits

One parfait provides 0.5 oz. GB, 0.5 oz. MMA and ½ cup FR for a 3-5 year old at breakfast

Lunch

Tropical Turkey Meatloaf

½ cup chopped green bell peppers
½ cup chopped onions
2 eggs, beaten
1 cup breadcrumbs
¾ cup pineapple tidbits, drained
1 teaspoon dried leaf basil
¾ teaspoon salt
½ teaspoon black pepper
½ teaspoon garlic powder
¼ teaspoon dried thyme
1¼ pounds ground turkey

1. Preheat oven to 350°. Coat small loaf pan with non-stick cooking spray.

2. Place green peppers and onions in a skillet over medium-high heat and sauté for 5 minutes.

3. Stir together eggs, breadcrumbs, pineapple, green pepper mixture and spices.

4. Add ground turkey and mix well by hand.

5. Spoon turkey mixture into loaf pan, packing loosely but evenly.

6. Bake for 65-90 minutes or until a meat thermometer inserted in center of loaf reads 165°. Remove from oven and rest it 5 minutes before cutting into 6 slices.

Makes 6 slices

¾ slice provides 1.5 oz. MMA for a 3-5 year old at lunch/supper

Breakfast

Whole Grain Toast, Blueberries, Milk

	Toddler	Pre-School	School Age
Toast	1/2 slice	1/2 slice	1 slice
Blueberries	1/4 cup	1/2 cup	1/2 cup
Milk	1/2 cup	3/4 cup	1 cup

Lunch

Super Italian Pasta, Bananas, Milk

	Toddler	Pre-School	School Age
Pasta*	1 cup	1-1/4 cups	1-3/4 cups
Banana	1/2	1	1
Milk	1/2 cup	3/4 cup	1 cup

Snack

Grand Pear Gondolas, Milk

	Toddler	Pre-School	School Age
Pear Gondolas*	2 gondolas	2 gondolas	3 gondolas
Milk	1/2 cup	1/2 cup	1 cup

twist & sprout

Lunch

Super Italian Pasta

9 ounces cooked chicken, chopped
6 ounces cooked whole grain pasta,
    spiral shaped
½ pound yellow onions, diced
⅔ cup chickpeas, rinsed and drained
1 teaspoon fresh garlic, minced
1 teaspoon olive oil
¾ cup zucchini, diced
¾ cup carrots, diced
1½ cups low-sodium marinara sauce
2¼ teaspoons dried Italian seasoning
⅛ teaspoon black pepper
3 tablespoons Parmesan cheese

1. Preheat oven to 350 degrees. Grease large casserole dish.

2. In large bowl, combine all ingredients. Transfer to casserole dish and cover with lid or parchment paper and foil.

3. Bake until carrots are tender and mixture is hot, about 30 to 45 minutes.

Makes 7½ cups

 1¼ cup provides 1 oz. GB, 1.5 oz. MMA and
 ½ cup VEG for a 3-5 year old at lunch/supper

Snack

Grand Pear Gondolas

3 pears (1 lb.) each pear cut into 4 wedges
    (12 wedges total)
6 1-ounce slices Colby cheese, cut in half
12 cherry tomatoes
12 toothpicks

1. Lay pears skin side down. Stack ingredients on each fruit piece as follows: 2 slices Colby and cherry tomato.

2. Fasten together with a toothpick.

Makes 12 gondolas

 2 gondolas provide 1 oz. MMA and
 ½ cup FR for a 3-5 year old at snack

Breakfast

Poofy Puffy Pancake, Plums, Milk

	Toddler	Pre-School	School Age
Pancake*	1 slice	1 slice	2 slices
Plums	1/4 cup	1/2 cup	1/2 cup
Milk	1/2 cup	3/4 cup	1 cup

Lunch

Pumped Up Red Peppers, Zippy Cucumbers, Peaches, Milk

	Toddler	Pre-School	School Age
Stuffed Peppers*	1/2 pepper	1 pepper	1 pepper
Cucumbers	1/8 cup	1/8 cup	1/8 cup
Peaches	1/8 cup	1/4 cup	1/4 cup
Milk	1/2 cup	3/4 cup	1 cup

Snack

Sassy Sweet Potato Fries, Milk

	Toddler	Pre-School	School Age
Sweet Potato Fries*	1/2 cup	1/2 cup	3/4 cup
Milk	1/2 cup	1/2 cup	1 cup

twist & sprout

AUTUMN Week 3 Wednesday

Breakfast

Poofy Puffy Pancakes

1½ tablespoons unsalted butter
1½ tablespoons olive oil
3 eggs
½ cup 1% or fat-free milk
¼ teaspoon vanilla extract
½ cup whole wheat flour
⅛ teaspoon salt

1. Preheat oven to 450 degrees.

2. Place the butter and oil in an oven-proof skillet. Put skillet in oven while it preheats.

3. In a small bowl, beat the eggs until frothy. Stir in milk, vanilla, flour and salt and mix well.

4. When oven is hot, remove the skillet and quickly tilt it to coat the bottom with the hot butter and oil.

5. Pour the batter into the hot skillet and then return it to the oven.

6. Bake until very puffy and golden-brown around the edge, around 20 to 25 minutes. Cut into 6 slices.

Makes 6 slices

   1 slice provides 0.5 oz. GB
   for a 3-5 year old at breakfast

Lunch

Pumped Up Red Peppers

3 red bell peppers, (1 lb.) halved lengthwise, stems and seeds removed
½ cup green onions, chopped
¾ teaspoon fresh garlic, minced
3 cups fresh baby spinach, packed
¾ cup tomato sauce
12 ounces cooked chicken, in bite-sized pieces
3 cups cooked brown rice, hot
3 tablespoons Parmesan cheese
Water for baking dish

1. Preheat the oven to 375 degrees. Coat a baking dish with non-stick cooking spray.

2. Heat large sauté pan and add the green onions, garlic, spinach and tomato sauce. Cook for 5 minutes.

3. Add chicken and rice and combine well.

4. Place halved peppers in baking dish. Fill with chicken/rice mixture and top with cheese.

5. Place baking dish in oven. Pour water into the baking dish, about halfway up the sides of the peppers.

6. Bake until peppers are soft, 30 to 40 minutes.

Makes 6 stuffed peppers

   1 stuffed pepper provides 1 oz. GB,
   2 oz. MMA and ½ cup VEG
   for a 3-5 year old at lunch/supper

Snack

Sassy Sweet Potato Fries

2 pounds sweet potatoes, peeled and cut into thin sticks
½ cup olive oil
½ tablespoon sugar
1 teaspoon salt
½ tablespoon turmeric

1. Preheat oven to 450 degrees. Line a baking sheet with foil or parchment paper.

2. In a large bowl, toss the sweet potatoes with the olive oil. Sprinkle with salt, sugar and spices and mix thoroughly.

3. Spread the sweet potatoes in a single layer on the lined baking sheet. Bake for 15 minutes. Stir and turn over potatoes and then continue cooking until browned, about 10 to 15 minutes longer.

Makes 3 cups

   ½ cup provides ½ cup VEG
   for a 3-5 year old at snack

AUTUMN Week 3 Thursday

Breakfast

Whole Grain Cereal, Scrambled Eggs, Banana, Milk

	Toddler	Pre-School	School Age
Cereal	1/2 cup	1/2 cup	1 cup
Eggs	1/4 cup	1/4 cup	1/2 cup
Banana	1/2	1	1
Milk	1/2 cup	3/4 cup	1 cup

Lunch

Marvelous Hummus Sandwich, Carrot Sticks, Honeydew Melon, Milk

	Toddler	Pre-School	School Age
Sandwich*	1/2 sandwich	1/2 sandwich	1 sandwich
Carrot Sticks	1/8 cup	1/8 cup	1/4 cup
Honeydew	1/8 cup	1/4 cup	1/4 cup
Milk	1/2 cup	3/4 cup	1 cup

Snack

Curry Yogurt Dip, Celery Sticks

	Toddler	Pre-School	School Age
Curry Yogurt Dip*	1/4 cup	1/4 cup	1/2 cup
Celery Sticks	1/2 cup	1/2 cup	3/4 cup

twist & sprout

Lunch

Marvelous Hummus Sandwich

6 slices whole wheat bread
½ cup hummus
3 tablespoons guacamole
3 romaine lettuce leaves
6 1-ounce slices mozzarella cheese
¾ cup cucumbers, sliced
¾ cup tomatoes, sliced

1. Toast the bread.

2. Spread 2 tablespoons of hummus and 1 tablespoon guacamole on three slices of toast.

3. Top each with 1 lettuce leaf, 2 slices cheese and the cucumber and tomato slices.

4. Top with second slice of toasted bread.

Makes 3 sandwiches

½ sandwich provides 1 oz. GB, 1.5 oz. MMA and ¼ cup VEG or a 3-5 year old at lunch/ supper

Snack

Curry Yogurt Dip

1½ cups plain low-fat yogurt
1 teaspoon curry powder
¼ teaspoon ground cumin
½ teaspoon sugar
½ teaspoon lemon juice

1. Combine all ingredients and stir to mix.

Makes 1½ cups

¼ cup provides 0.5 oz. MMA for a 3-5 year old at snack

Breakfast

Awesome Oatmeal, Fruit Topping, Milk

	Toddler	Pre-School	School Age
Oatmeal*	1/4 cup	1/4 cup	1/2 cup
Fruit Topping*	1/4 cup	1/2 cup	1/2 cup
Milk	1/2 cup	3/4 cup	1 cup

Lunch

Mighty Meatballs with Rock'n Ragu Sauce, Whole Wheat Roll, Broccoli Crowns, Mixed Fruit, Milk

	Toddler	Pre-School	School Age
Meatballs*	3	4	6
Roll	1/2 roll	1/2 roll	1 roll
Broccoli	1/8 cup	1/4 cup	1/2 cup
Mixed Fruit	1/8 cup	1/4 cup	1/4 cup
Milk	1/2 cup	3/4 cup	1 cup

Snack

Apple Slices, Cheese Stick

	Toddler	Pre-School	School Age
String Cheese (1 oz.)	1/2 stick	1/2 stick	1 stick
Apple Slices	1/2 cup	1/2 cup	3/4 cup

twist & sprout

132

Breakfast

Awesome Oatmeal

1½ cups water
¾ cup regular rolled oats
⅛ teaspoon ground cinnamon
1½ cups pineapple, drained, diced
1½ cups mango, chopped
4 tablespoons walnuts, chopped

1. In medium sauce pan, bring water and oats to a boil. Add cinnamon.

2. Simmer oats for 7-10 minutes or until thick. Remove from heat.

3. Top each serving of oatmeal with pineapple, mango and walnuts.

Makes 1½ cups oatmeal

¼ cup oatmeal and ½ cup fruit topping provide 0.5 oz. GB and ½ cup FR for a 3-5 year old at breakfast

Lunch

Mighty Meatballs with Rock'n Ragu Sauce

Sauce
⅛ cup onions, minced
2 teaspoons fresh garlic, minced
1 cup low-sodium marinara sauce
Meatballs
¾ pound ground beef (85/15)
1 egg
2 tablespoons water
⅓ cup breadcrumbs
¼ cup onions, minced
¼ teaspoon salt
⅛ teaspoon pepper
⅛ teaspoon dried basil

1. In small saucepan, sauté onions and garlic until tender, about 5 minutes. Add marinara sauce and simmer for 20 minutes. Set aside.

2. Preheat oven to 350 degrees. Line a baking sheet with foil or parchment paper, or coat with non-stick cooking spray.

3. In a large bowl, combine egg, water, breadcrumbs, onion, salt, pepper and basil.

4. Add ground beef, broken into chunks and mix together with your hands. Form into meatballs about 1-inch in diameter and place on the baking sheet.

4. Bake for 25-30 minutes, until meatballs are firm.

Makes 24 small meatballs

4 meatballs with ⅛ cup sauce provides 1.5 oz. MMA and ⅛ cup VEG for a 3-5 year old at lunch/supper

Breakfast

Green Machine Smoothie, Whole Grain Toast, Milk

	Toddler	Pre-School	School Age
Smoothie*	1/2 cup	3/4 cup	3/4 cup
Toast	1/2 slice	1/2 slice	1 slice
Milk	1/2 cup	3/4 cup	1 cup

Lunch

Buddy Bows & Veggies, Spinach Salad, Fruit Kabobs, Milk

	Toddler	Pre-School	School Age
Buddy Bows*	3/4 cup	3/4 cup	1-1/2 cups
Spinach Salad	1/4 cup	1/2 cup	1 cup
Fruit Kabobs	1/8 cup	1/4 cup	1/4 cup
Milk	1/2 cup	3/4 cup	1 cup

Snack

Goofy Grapes, Whole Grain Crackers

	Toddler	Pre-School	School Age
Crackers	3	3	6
Grapes	1/2 cup	1/2 cup	3/4 cup

twist & sprout

Breakfast

Green Machine Smoothies

3 cups 1% or fat-free milk
3 bananas (about 1 lb.) peeled and frozen
1½ avocados, peeled and pitted
3 cups spinach, loosely packed
2 cups green apples, cored and chopped

1. Blend all ingredients in blender until smooth.

Makes 4½ cups

¾ cup smoothie provides ½ cup FR/VEG
for a 3-5 year old at breakfast

Lunch

Buddy Bows & Veggies

1½ tablespoons olive oil
½ cup sweet onions, sliced
1½ cups broccoli, finely chopped
¾ cup bell peppers, any color, finely chopped
¼ teaspoon Italian seasoning
¾ cup kidney or black beans
1½ cups bowtie (farfalle) pasta, cooked
1½ cups cheddar cheese

1. Heat oil in large skillet on medium-high heat.

2. Add onions, broccoli, peppers and Italian seasoning. Cook for 5 minutes or until broccoli and onions are tender.

3. Stir in beans and cooked pasta. Cook until beans and pasta are heated through.

4. Add cheese and stir to combine.

Makes 4½ cups

¾ cup provides 0.5 GB, 1.5 oz. MMA and
¼ cup VEG for a 3-5 year old at lunch/supper

Breakfast

Viva La Veggie Scrambler, Whole
Grain Tortilla, Milk

	Toddler	Pre-School	School Age
Scrambler*	1/3 cup	2/3 cup	2/3 cup
Tortilla	1/2 tortilla	1/2 tortilla	1 tortilla
Milk	1/2 cup	3/4 cup	1 cup

Lunch

Hearty Pot Roast, Whole Grain Roll,
Cantaloupe, Milk

	Toddler	Pre-School	School Age
Pot Roast*	2/3 cup	1 cup	1-1/3 cups
Roll	1/2 roll	1/2 roll	1 roll
Cantaloupe	1/8 cup	1/4 cup	1/4 cup
Milk	1/2 cup	3/4 cup	1 cup

Snack

Monkey Ice, Milk

	Toddler	Pre-School	School Age
Monkey Ice*	1/2 cup	1/2 cup	3/4 cup
Milk	1/2 cup	1/2 cup	3/4 cup

twist & sprout

136

Breakfast

Viva La Veggie Scrambler

3 teaspoons olive oil
2 cups bell peppers, chopped
1½ cups mushrooms, sliced
6 eggs, beaten
¼ cup Parmesan cheese
3 8-inch whole grain tortillas

1. In medium sauté pan, heat oil over medium heat.

2. Add bell peppers and mushrooms and sauté for about 2 minutes.

3. Add eggs. Cook, stirring occasionally until firm, solid and not clear, about 2-3 minutes.

4. Stir in Parmesan cheese.

5. Serve with tortilla.

Makes 4 cups

 ⅔ cup provides 2 oz. MMA and ½ cup VEG
 for a 3-5 year old at breakfast

Lunch

Hearty Pot Roast

1 pound boneless beef chuck roast
1 cup potatoes, quartered
1 cup carrots, peeled and chopped
1 cup mushrooms, chopped
1 cup onions, chopped
2 large garlic cloves, minced
1 small tomato, chopped
2¼ cups low-sodium beef broth
1½ teaspoons dried Italian seasoning

1. Season chuck roast with salt and pepper.

2. Heat oil in heavy skillet. Brown the roast on all sides.

3. Place ingredients in slow cooker in this order: browned roast, potatoes, carrots, mushrooms, onions, garlic, tomato and beef broth.

4. Cook on high for one hour. Add Italian seasoning. Reduce heat to low and cook for 6 hours or overnight.

5. Cut beef into 6 pieces

Serves 6

 1 cup provides 1.5 oz. MMA and ½ cup VEG
 for a 3-5 year old at lunch/supper

Snack

Monkey Ice

6 large bananas, frozen
1½ teaspoons vanilla extract
1½ teaspoons ground cinnamon

1. Place bananas and vanilla in a food processor or blender. Process until they have a smooth, ice cream-like consistency.

2. Pour into glasses and sprinkle with cinnamon.

Makes 3 cups

 ½ cup provides ½ cup FR
 for a 3-5 year old at snack

Breakfast

Perky Pancakes, Orange Smiles, Milk

	Toddler	Pre-School	School Age
Pancakes*	1 pancake	1 pancake	2 pancakes
Oranges	1/4 cup	1/2 cup	1/2 cup
Milk	1/2 cup	3/4 cup	1 cup

Lunch

Pretzel Chicken, Whole Grain Bread, Bionic Brussels Sprouts, Peaches, Milk

	Toddler	Pre-School	School Age
Chicken*	1 piece	1 piece	1-1/2 pieces
Bread	1/2 slice	1/2 slice	1 slice
Brussels Sprouts*	1/8 cup	1/4 cup	1/2 cup
Peaches	1/8 cup	1/4 cup	1/4 cup
Milk	1/2 cup	3/4 cup	1 cup

Snack

Pretzel Rods, Sliced Plums

	Toddler	Pre-School	School Age
Pretzel Rods	2	2	3
Plums	1/2 cup	1/2 cup	3/4 cup

138

Breakfast

Perky Pancakes

½ cup whole wheat flour
½ teaspoon baking powder
⅛ teaspoon salt
1 egg
¼ cup 1% or fat-free milk
¾ cup cooked oatmeal
2 teaspoons vegetable oil

1. Heat large skillet over medium heat.

2. In a large bowl, combine flour, baking powder and salt.

3. In a separate bowl, whisk together egg, milk and oil. Stir in the cooked oatmeal until just incorporated.

4. Add oatmeal mixture to dry ingredients, stirring gently. Don't over-mix.

5. Pour batter into skillet. Cook on both sides.

Makes 12 small pancakes

  1 pancake provides 0.5 oz. GB
  for a 3-5 year old at breakfast

Lunch

Pretzel Chicken

1 pound boneless, skinless chicken breasts,
  cut into six portions
1 egg, beaten
¾ cup pretzels

1. Preheat oven to 350 degrees. Line a baking sheet with foil and coat with cooking spray.

2. Dip chicken in eggs and dredge in pretzels.

3. Place chicken pieces on baking sheet. Bake for 30 minutes or until internal temperature is 165 degrees.

4. Serve with honey-mustard sauce.

Makes 6 pieces

  1 piece provides 1.5 oz. MMA
  for a 3-5 year old at lunch/supper

Honey-Mustard Sauce

⅓ cup mayonnaise
1½ tablespoons yellow mustard
2 teaspoons Dijon mustard
1½ tablespoons honey
1 teaspoon lemon juice

1. In small bowl, whisk all ingredients together.

Makes ½ cup

Lunch

Bionic Brussels Sprouts

1½ pounds Brussels sprouts,
  cut in half lengthwise
2 tablespoons olive oil
⅛ teaspoon salt

1. Preheat oven to 350 degrees. Line baking sheet with foil or parchment paper.

2. In a large bowl, toss Brussels sprouts with the olive oil and salt. Place on lined baking sheet in a single layer.

3. Roast for 30 minutes or until Brussels sprouts are tender and outer leaves are browned and crisp.

Makes 3 cups

  ¼ cup provides ¼ cup VEG
  for a 3-5 year old at lunch/supper

AUTUMN Week 4 Thursday

Breakfast

Sunshine Muffins, Grapes, Milk

	Toddler	Pre-School	School Age
Muffin*	1/2 muffin	1/2 muffin	1 muffin
Grapes	1/4 cup	1/2 cup	1/2 cup
Milk	1/2 cup	3/4 cup	1 cup

Lunch

Tasty Turkey Tomato Bites, Brown Rice Pilaf, Tiny Tasty Edamame, Milk

	Toddler	Pre-School	School Age
Turkey Bites*	1 bite	1 bite	2 bites
Rice Pilaf*	1/4 cup	1/4 cup	1/2 cup
Edamame	1/8 cup	1/4 cup	1/4 cup
Milk	1/2 cup	3/4 cup	1 cup

Snack

Blast Off Black Bean Dip, Carrot Sticks

	Toddler	Pre-School	School Age
Bean Dip*	2 tbsp	2 tbsp	1/4 cup
Carrot Sticks	1/2 cup	1/2 cup	3/4 cup

twist & sprout

Breakfast

Sunshine Muffins

1 cup whole wheat flour
¾ teaspoon baking powder
¼ teaspoon baking soda
¼ teaspoon ground cinnamon
⅛ teaspoon ground nutmeg
⅛ teaspoon salt
1 cup apples, cored and finely chopped
1 teaspoon honey
1 egg
¼ cup 1% or fat-free milk
⅛ cup vegetable oil

1. Preheat oven to 400 degrees. Lightly grease a 6-cup muffin pan or line with paper cups.
2. In a large bowl, combine flour, baking powder, baking soda, cinnamon, nutmeg and salt. Make a well in center of flour mixture.
3. In another bowl, mix together the honey, egg, milk and oil. Stir in apples.
4. Add wet mixture to flour mixture all at once. Stir until moistened.
5. Spoon batter into muffin cups. Bake for 18-20 minutes or until golden brown.

Makes 6 muffins

  ½ muffin provides 0.5 oz. GB
  for a 3-5 year old at breakfast

Lunch

Tasty Turkey Tomato Bites

3 small potatoes, halved
2 small tomatoes, each cut into 3 slices
6 ounces cooked turkey, sliced
¾ cup (3 ounces) mozzarella cheese, shredded

1. Preheat oven to 400 degrees. Line a small baking pan with foil or coat with non-stick spray.
2. Cut potatoes in half and season with olive oil, salt and pepper. Roast until tender, about 25-35 minutes. Stirring halfway through baking.
3. Remove potatoes from oven. On each potato half, stack one tomato slice, 1 ounce turkey and 2 tablespoons cheese.
4. Return potatoes to oven until cheese melts, about 3 minutes.

Makes 6 bites

  1 bite provides 1.5 oz. MMA and ¼ cup VEG
  for a 3-5 year old at lunch/supper

Brown Rice Pilaf

½ cup long grain brown rice
½ cup long grain enriched white rice
1½ cups low-sodium chicken broth
1½ tablespoons onions, finely diced
⅛ teaspoon black or white pepper

1. In a stockpot, place all ingredients and bring to a boil.
2. Reduce heat, cover and simmer for 40 minutes.

Makes 2 cups

  ¼ cup provides 0.5 oz. GB
  for a 3-5 year old at lunch/supper

Snack

Blast Off Black Bean Dip

1 15-ounce can black beans,
  rinsed and drained
½ small tomato, diced
½ large garlic clove, minced
1½ teaspoons lime juice
½ teaspoon cumin
⅛ teaspoon salt

1. In a medium bowl, stir together all ingredients. Mash well.

Makes 1 cup

  2 tablespoons provides 0.5 oz. MMA
  for a 3-5 year old at snack

Breakfast

Breakfast Burrito Swirls, Apple Fans, Milk

	Toddler	Pre-School	School Age
Swirls*	1 swirl	1 swirl	2 swirls
Apple Fans	1/4 cup	1/2 cup	1/2 cup
Milk	1/2 cup	3/4 cup	1 cup

Lunch

Silly Dilly Chicken Soup, Whole Grain Crackers, Pineapple, Milk

	Toddler	Pre-School	School Age
Chicken Soup*	1 cup	1-1/2 cups	2 cups
Crackers	3	3	6
Pineapple	1/8 cup	1/4 cup	1/4 cup
Milk	1/2 cup	3/4 cup	1 cup

Snack

Mini Trees, String Cheese

	Toddler	Pre-School	School Age
Broccoli Trees	1/2 cup	1/2 cup	3/4 cup
String Cheese 1 oz.	1/2 stick	1/2 stick	1 stick

142

Breakfast

Breakfast Burrito Swirls

1 cup spinach leaves, loosely packed
6 eggs, lightly beaten
1½ tablespoons water
3 8-inch whole wheat tortillas, cut in half

1. Coat skillet with cooking spray. Sauté spinach until wilted. Remove from pan.

2. Whisk eggs and water together and then pour into the hot skillet. Add spinach.

3. Cook eggs in one piece by lifting edges to let raw egg run onto hot pan. Flip the whole piece, so you have a large "fried egg." Cut into six wedges.

4. Place one wedge on each half tortilla and roll up.

Makes 6 swirls

1 swirl provides 0.5 oz. GB and 2 oz. MMA for a 3-5 year old at breakfast

Lunch

Silly Dilly Chicken Soup

2 tablespoons olive oil
1 cup diced yellow onions
2½ cups carrots, peeled and sliced
2 cups celery, chopped
1 cup mushrooms, chopped
1 pound boneless, skinless chicken breast
1 quart low-sodium chicken broth
1 cup baby spinach, finely chopped
1 tablespoon parsley
1½ cups cooked brown rice
2 teaspoons lemon juice, or to taste

1. Cut chicken in ½ inch cubes.

2. In soup kettle, heat olive oil over medium heat. Add onions, carrots, celery, and mushrooms and sauté about 2 minutes.

3. Move vegetables to one side of the pan. Add chicken and sauté until chicken is lightly golden brown, about 5 minutes.

4. Add broth and bring to boil. Reduce heat and simmer until chicken is cooked through and tender, about 20 minutes.

5. Add spinach, parsley and rice and cook until rice is heated through.

6. Season with lemon juice, as desired.

Makes 9 cups

1½ cups provides 0.5 oz. GB, 1.5 oz. MMA and ½ cup VEG for a 3-5 year old at lunch/supper

Winter Recipes

Soup

WINTER Week 1 Monday

Breakfast

Crazy Corn Cakes, Fruit, Milk

	Toddler	Pre-School	School Age
Corn Cakes*	1 pancake	1 pancake	2 pancakes
Fruit	1/4 cup	1/2 cup	1/2 cup
Milk	1/2 cup	3/4 cup	1 cup

Lunch

Pizazz Pocket Pizza, Green Pepper Squares, Bananas, Milk

	Toddler	Pre-School	School Age
Pocket Pizza*	1/2 pocket	1 pocket	1 pocket
Green Peppers	1/8 cup	1/8 cup	1/4 cup
Bananas	1/8 cup	1/4 cup	1/4 cup
Milk	1/2 cup	3/4 cup	1 cup

Snack

Whole Grain Crackers, Grapes

	Toddler	Pre-School	School Age
Crackers	3	3	6
Grapes	1/2 cup	1/2 cup	3/4 cup

Breakfast

Crazy Corn Cakes

1 cup whole wheat flour
1 teaspoon baking powder
¼ teaspoon salt
1 egg
½ cup 1% or fat-free milk
1½ cups whole kernel corn, thawed or drained
1 tablespoon vegetable oil
3 cups fresh or frozen fruit, chopped

1. In a large bowl, combine flour, baking powder and salt.

2. In a separate bowl, whisk together egg and milk. Stir in the corn kernels.

3. Mix corn mixture with dry ingredients, stirring gently.

4. Heat oil in large skillet over medium heat.

5. Pour batter into hot skillet. Cook until bubbles form on the top, about 2-3 minutes. Flip pancakes and cook until browned on each side, 2-3 minutes more.

6. Top with fresh fruit.

Makes 16 pancakes

1 pancake provides 0.5 oz. GB, topped with ½ cup FR for a 3-5 year old at breakfast

Lunch

Pizazz Pocket Pizzas

1 cup spinach
8 ounces ricotta cheese
1½ cups tomatoes, chopped
1 cup tomato sauce
2 15-ounce cans (3 cups) northern or cannellini beans, rinsed and drained
3 8-inch whole wheat pita rounds

1. Preheat oven to 350 degrees. Line baking sheet with lightly greased foil.

2. In a large bowl, stir together spinach, ricotta cheese, tomatoes, tomato sauce and beans.

3. Cut pita rounds in half, then slice open the pockets. Divide filling equally, stuff the 6 pockets and place on baking sheet.

4. Bake in oven for 8 to 10 minutes.

Makes 6 pocket pizzas

1 pocket pizza provides 1 oz. GB, 2 oz. MMA and ¼ cup VEG for a 3-5 year old at lunch/supper.

Breakfast

Super Power Oatmeal, Hard Boiled Egg, Blueberries, Milk

	Toddler	Pre-School	School Age
Oatmeal*	1/3 cup	1/3 cup	2/3 cup
Egg	1/2 egg	1/2 egg	1 egg
Blueberries	1/4 cup	1/2 cup	1/2 cup
Milk	1/2 cup	3/4 cup	1 cup

Lunch

Aloha Tuna Melt Sandwich, Chimney Chili Carrots, Milk

	Toddler	Pre-School	School Age
Tuna Melt*	1/2 sandwich	1 sandwich	1 sandwich
Carrots*	1/8 cup	1/4 cup	1/2 cup
Milk	1/2 cup	3/4 cup	1 cup

Snack

Apple Wedges, Milk

	Toddler	Pre-School	School Age
Apple	1/2 cup	1/2 cup	3/4 cup
Milk	1/2 cup	1/2 cup	1 cup

Breakfast

Super Power Oatmeal

¾ cup regular rolled oats
1½ cups water
1 teaspoon ground cinnamon
¾ teaspoon vanilla extract
2 teaspoons brown sugar
¾ cup fresh or frozen blueberries, thawed

1. In a large saucepan, combine oats, water and cinnamon.

2. Bring oatmeal to a boil. Reduce heat and simmer for 7 to 10 minutes, or until mixture has thickened.

3. Mix in vanilla, brown sugar and blueberries. Heat until blueberries are warm.

Makes 2 cups

⅓ cup provides 0.5 oz. GB
for a 3-5 year old at breakfast

Lunch

Aloha Tuna Melt Sandwiches

¼ cup onions, chopped
¾ cup celery, chopped
¾ cup red bell peppers, diced
2 5-ounce cans water-packed tuna
2 teaspoons mayonnaise
2 teaspoons mustard
¼ teaspoon dried leaf thyme
Dash black pepper
6 slices whole grain bread
¾ cup cheddar cheese, shredded
6 pineapple rings

1. Preheat oven to 350 degrees.

2. In medium bowl, combine vegetables, tuna, mayonnaise, mustard and spices.

3. Place bread slices on a baking sheet. Top each slice with tuna salad, 2 tablespoons of cheese and one pineapple ring.

4. Bake until cheese is melted, about 10 minutes.

Makes 6 tuna melt sandwiches

1 tuna melt provides 1 oz. GB,
2 oz. MMA and ¼ cup VEG
for a 3-5 year old at lunch/supper

Lunch

Chimney Chili Carrots

1¾ cup carrots, peeled and cut in small chunks
  (baby carrots are fine)
½ teaspoon chili powder
¼ cup onions, minced
1 teaspoon lime juice
2 teaspoons olive oil

1. Preheat oven to 350 degrees. Line a baking sheet with foil or parchment paper.

2. Mix all ingredients together and place in a single layer on baking sheet.

3. Roast until lightly golden and tender, not mushy, about 20 to 30 minutes.

Makes 1½ cups

¼ cup provides ¼ cup VEG
for a 3-5 year old at lunch/supper

WINTER Week 1 Wednesday

Breakfast

Whole Grain English Muffin, Nutty Nut Butter, Orange Smiles, Milk

	Toddler	Pre-School	School Age
English Muffin	1/2 muffin	1/2 muffin	1 muffin
Nut Butter	1 tbsp	1 tbsp	2 tbsp
Oranges	1/4 cup	1/2 cup	1/2 cup
Milk	1/2 cup	3/4 cup	1 cup

Lunch

Cheesy Butternut Mac, Broccoli Trees, Pears, Milk

	Toddler	Pre-School	School Age
Cheesy Mac*	2/3 cup	1 cup	1-1/3 cups
Broccoli	1/8 cup	1/8 cup	1/4 cup
Pears	1/8 cup	1/4 cup	1/4 cup
Milk	1/2 cup	3/4 cup	1 cup

Snack

Stuffed Celery, Milk

	Toddler	Pre-School	School Age
Stuffed Celery*	6 sticks	6 sticks	9 sticks
Milk	1/2 cup	1/2 cup	1 cup

twist & sprout

Lunch

Cheesy Butternut Mac

2¼ cups (1#) butternut squash, peeled, cubed
6 ounces macaroni
2 teaspoons butter
¾ cup mushrooms, sliced
½ cup green onions, thinly sliced
1½ tablespoons flour
¾ cup 1% or fat-free milk
⅛ teaspoon salt
⅛ teaspoon ground black pepper
2¼ cups shredded cheese

1. Preheat oven to 350 degrees. Grease a baking dish.

2. In a medium saucepan, boil squash in water until tender. Drain.

3. Cook pasta according to directions. Drain.

4. In medium saucepan, sauté mushrooms and green onions in butter until tender.

5. Sprinkle flour over mushroom mixture. Cook and stir for 1 minute.

6. Add milk, salt and pepper to mushroom mixture. Cook and stir over medium heat until thickened. Remove from heat.

7. Stir pasta into the mushroom mixture.

Lunch

8. Spoon half of the mushroom-pasta mixture into the prepared baking dish, top with half of the cooked squash and sprinkle with half of the cheese. Repeat layers, ending with the cheese on top.

9. Bake, uncovered, until cheese is melted, about 20 to 25 minutes.

Makes 6 cups

  1 cup provides 1 oz. GB,
  1.5 oz. MMA and ½ cup VEG
  for a 3-5 year old at lunch/supper

Snack

Stuffed Celery

36 4-inch long celery sticks
¾ cup (6 ounces) cream cheese
⅓ cup raisins

1. Spread cream cheese on celery sticks.

2. Top with raisins.

Makes 36 stuffed celery sticks

  6 celery sticks provide ½ cup VEG
  for a 3-5 year old at snack

WINTER Week 1 Thursday

Breakfast

Whole Grain Toast, Banana, Milk

	Toddler	Pre-School	School Age
Toast	1/2 slice	1/2 slice	1 slice
Banana	1/2	1	1
Milk	1/2 cup	3/4 cup	1 cup

Lunch

Chill 'n Chili, Whole Grain Crackers, Honeydew Drops, Milk

	Toddler	Pre-School	School Age
Chili*	2/3 cup	1 cup	1-1/3 cups
Crackers	3	3	6
Honey Dew Melon	1/8 cup	1/4 cup	1/4 cup
Milk	1/2 cup	3/4 cup	1 cup

Snack

Peaches, Yogurt

	Toddler	Pre-School	School Age
Peaches	1/2 cup	1/2 cup	3/4 cup
Yogurt	1/4 cup	1/4 cup	1/2 cup

twist & sprout

Lunch

Chill'n Chili

½ tablespoon olive oil
½ cup yellow onions, chopped medium
½ cup green bell peppers, chopped
1 teaspoon fresh garlic, minced
½ tablespoon chili powder
¼ teaspoon paprika
1 cup (½#) butternut squash, peeled, diced
2 15-ounce cans (3 cups) black beans,
  rinsed and drained
¾ cup water
1 cup whole kernel corn, thawed or drained
1 14½-ounce can stewed tomatoes

1. In a large non-stick skillet, heat oil over medium heat. Add onions, bell peppers and garlic. Cover and cook 5 minutes.

2. Add chili powder and paprika. Cook 1 minute, stirring constantly.

3. Place onion mixture in slow cooker. Mix in the squash, beans, water, corn and tomatoes.

4. Cover and cook on low for 8 hours or until chili is thick. Note: Cooking on high will take less time, but be careful not to scorch the chili on the bottom of the pot.

Makes 6 cups

1 cup provides 1.5 oz. MMA and ½ cup VEG for a 3-5 year old at lunch/supper

153

Breakfast

Eggerific Muffin Sandwich, Apple Wedges, Milk

	Toddler	Pre-School	School Age
Eggerific Sandwich*	1/2 sandwich	1/2 sandwich	1 sandwich
Apples	1/4 cup	1/2 cup	1/2 cup
Milk	1/2 cup	3/4 cup	1 cup

Lunch

Lotta Veggie Turkey Sammie, Groovy Green Beans, Peaches, Milk

	Toddler	Pre-School	School Age
Pocket Sandwich*	1/2 pocket	1 pocket	1 pocket
Green Beans	1/8 cup	1/8 cup	1/4 cup
Peaches	1/8 cup	1/4 cup	1/4 cup
Milk	1/2 cup	3/4 cup	1 cup

Snack

Winter King's Cottage Cheese, Carrot Spears

	Toddler	Pre-School	School Age
Cottage Cheese*	1/2 cup	1/2 cup	1 cup
Carrots	1/2 cup	1/2 cup	3/4 cup

Breakfast

Eggerific Muffin Sandwich

3 eggs
3 whole grain English muffins, split
1½ tablespoons butter
1 medium tomato, thinly sliced
¾ cup baby spinach

1. Coat frying pan with non-stick cooking spray, then heat over medium heat.

2. Crack eggs into pan and cook for 3 minutes or until set. Turn over and cook for 30 seconds. Remove from heat.

3. Toast muffins until crisp and spread lightly with butter.

4. Top 3 muffin halves with spinach, tomato and 1 egg. Top with remaining muffin halves.

Makes 3 muffin sandwiches

½ muffin sandwich provides 0.5 oz. GB, 2 oz. MMA for a 6-12 year old at breakfast

Lunch

Lotta Veggie Turkey Sammies

1 teaspoon olive oil
½ cup yellow onions, chopped
1½ cup red or green bell peppers, sliced
½ cup spinach, cooked
  (or thawed with water squeezed out)
3 8-inch whole wheat pita rounds
½ cup part-skim ricotta cheese
12 ounces turkey breast,
  cooked and cut into strips

1. In non-stick skillet, heat oil and sauté onions and bell peppers until tender.

2. Add spinach and cook until warmed through.

3. Cut each pita round in half, then slice open the pockets. Fill each with 1 tablespoon ricotta cheese, ½ cup spinach, ½ cup onion/pepper mixture and 2 ounces of turkey.

Makes 6 pita pocket sandwiches

1 pocket sandwich provides 1 oz. GB, 2 oz. MMA and ¼ cup VEG for a 3-5 year old at lunch/supper

Snack

Winter King's Cottage Cheese

12 ounces cottage cheese
1½ cups fresh or frozen blueberries, thawed

1. Stir together cottage cheese and blueberries.

Makes 3 cups

½ cup provides 1 oz. MMA and ¼ cup FR

Breakfast

Superstar Breakfast, Milk

	Toddler	Pre-School	School Age
Cereal with Fruit*	3/4 cup	3/4 cup	1-1/2 cups
Milk	1/2 cup	3/4 cup	1 cup

Lunch

Cheesy Chicken Quesadilla, Cauliflower Clouds, Mandarin Bursts, Milk

	Toddler	Pre-School	School Age
Quesadillas*	1/2 quesadilla	1 quesadilla	1 quesadilla
Cauliflower	1/8 cup	1/8 cup	1/4 cup
Mandarin Oranges	1/8 cup	1/4 cup	1/4 cup
Milk	1/2 cup	3/4 cup	1 cup

Snack

Apple Boats, Milk

	Toddler	Pre-School	School Age
Apple Boats	1/2 cup	1/2 cup	3/4 cup
Milk	1/2 cup	1/2 cup	1 cup

Breakfast

Superstar Breakfast

2 cups water
1½ teaspoons pumpkin pie spice
¾ cup dry whole grain or enriched couscous
3½ cups pears, chopped

1. In medium saucepan, combine water and pumpkin pie spice. Bring to a boil.

2. Stir in couscous and pears. Cover and remove from heat.

3. Let stand for 5 minutes.

Makes 4 cups

¾ cup provides 0.5 oz. GB and ½ cup FR for a 3-5 year old at breakfast

Lunch

Cheesy Chicken Quesadillas

9 ounces cooked chicken, finely chopped
1 teaspoon oil
¼ cup onions, chopped
1 cup mushrooms, sliced
1 cup broccoli, finely chopped
¾ cup refried beans
6 8-inch whole grain tortillas
3 tablespoons taco sauce
¾ cup mozzarella cheese

1. Preheat oven to 350 degrees. Line a baking sheet with foil or parchment paper, or coat with cooking spray.

2. In a saucepan, heat oil and sauté onions, mushrooms and broccoli until tender.

3. Add refried beans and heat through.

4. Place tortillas on baking sheet. Spread each with ½ cup of the bean vegetable mixture and top with 1 teaspoon taco sauce (or to taste), 1½ ounces chicken and 2 tablespoons cheese. Fold tortilla in half.

5. Bake in oven until cheese is melted, about 5-7 minutes.

Makes 6 quesadillas

1 quesadilla provides 1 oz. GB, 2 oz. MMA and ¼ cup VEG for a 3-5 year old at lunch/supper

WINTER Week 2 Tuesday

Breakfast

Creamy Apple Wrap, Milk

	Toddler	Pre-School	School Age
Apple Wraps*	1 wrap	2 wraps	2 wraps
Milk	1/2 cup	3/4 cup	1 cup

Lunch

Sassy Salmon, Awesome Asian Rice, Lovely Little Peas, Peppy Pineapple, Milk

	Toddler	Pre-School	School Age
Salmon*	1 fillet	1-1/2 fillets	2 fillets
Rice*	1/4 cup	1/4 cup	1/2 cup
Peas	1/8 cup	1/4 cup	1/2 cup
Pineapple	1/8 cup	1/4 cup	1/4 cup
Milk	1/2 cup	3/4 cup	1 cup

Snack

Hummus, Bell Pepper Strips

	Toddler	Pre-School	School Age
Hummus*	2 tbsp	2 tbsp	1/4 cup
Bell Pepper Strips	1/2 cup	1/2 cup	3/4 cup

Breakfast

Creamy Apple Wraps

6 8-inch whole wheat tortillas
12 tablespoons nut butter
3 cups apples, thinly sliced

1. Spread 2 tablespoons nut butter on each tortilla.
2. Top each tortilla with ½ cup apple slices.
3. Roll up tortillas and cut in half.

Makes 12 wraps

2 wraps provide 1 oz. GB, 1 oz. MMA and ½ cup FR for a 3-5 year old at breakfast

Lunch

Awesome Asian Rice

1½ cups hot cooked brown rice
1½ tablespoons low-sodium soy sauce
1 teaspoon sugar
1 teaspoon garlic powder
1 teaspoon black pepper
1 teaspoon ground ginger

1. Mix all ingredients together.

Makes 1½ cups

¼ cup provides 0.5 oz. GB
for a 3-5 year old at lunch/supper

Lunch

Sassy Salmon

14 ounces salmon filets
2 tablespoons honey
1 tablespoon low-sodium soy sauce
1 tablespoon orange juice
2 tablespoons olive oil

1. Preheat oven to 375 degrees. Line a baking sheet with foil or parchment paper. Cut salmon into 9 equal pieces.
2. In small bowl, mix honey, soy sauce, orange juice and olive oil. Set aside.
3. Place filets on baking sheet and spoon the honey mixture over them
4. Place baking sheet on middle oven rack. Bake until fish is firm, about 7-10 minutes.

Makes 9 filets

1½ filets provide 1.5 oz. MMA
for a 3-5 year old at lunch/supper

Snack

Hummus

1 15-ounce can (1½ cups) chickpeas, rinsed and drained
2½ tablespoons olive oil
2 tablespoons fresh lemon juice
2 cloves fresh garlic, minced
⅛ teaspoon ground cumin
⅛ teaspoon salt or to taste

1. Place all ingredients in blender or food processor. Process until smooth.
2. Adjust seasoning as needed.

Makes 1 cup

2 tablespoons provide 0.5 oz. MMA
for a 3-5 year old at snack

Breakfast

Big Dipper Parfait, Milk

	Toddler	Pre-School	School Age
Berries*	1/4 cup	1/2 cup	1/2 cup
Yogurt*	1/4 cup	1/4 cup	1/2 cup
Granola*	1/8 cup	1/8 cup	1/4 cup
Milk	1/2 cup	3/4 cup	1 cup

Lunch

Fun Frijole Wraps, Broccoli Trees, Apple Cubes, Milk

	Toddler	Pre-School	School Age
Wraps*	1 wrap	2 wraps	2 wraps
Broccoli	1/8 cup	1/8 cup	1/4 cup
Apples	1/8 cup	1/4 cup	1/4 cup
Milk	1/2 cup	3/4 cup	1 cup

Snack

All-Star Snack, Milk

	Toddler	Pre-School	School Age
All-Star Snack*	1/2 cup	1/2 cup	3/4 cup
Milk	1/2 cup	1/2 cup	1 cup

WINTER Week 2 Wednesday

Breakfast

Big Dipper Parfaits

3 cups frozen mixed berries
3 cups plain low-fat yogurt
1 cup granola

1. In single-serving bowls or glasses, layer ½ cup fruit, ¼ cup yogurt and ⅛ cup granola to make each parfait.

Makes 6 parfaits

1 parfait provides 0.5 oz. GB, 0.5 oz. MMA and ½ cup FR for a 3-5 year old at breakfast

Lunch

Fun Frijole Wraps

1½ cups avocado, mashed
2 15-ounce cans (3 cups) black beans, rinsed and drained
2 tablespoons fresh garlic, minced
2 teaspoons ground cumin
½ teaspoon chili powder
1 tablespoon lemon or lime juice
⅛ teaspoon salt
⅛ teaspoon ground black pepper
6 8-inch whole grain tortillas
1 cup tomatoes, sliced
2 cups spinach, chopped
½ cup cheese, shredded

1. In a large bowl, combine avocados, black beans, garlic, cumin, chili powder, lime juice, salt and pepper and then mash with a fork until smooth.
2. Spread each tortilla with ¾ cup bean mixture. Top with tomatoes, cheese and spinach.
3. Roll up each tortilla and cut in half.

Makes 12 wraps

2 wraps provide 1 oz. GB, 2 oz. MMA and ½ cup VEG for a 3-5 year old at lunch/supper

Snack

All-Star Snack

1 cup water, divided
1½ cups carrots, peeled and sliced
¾ cup sweet potatoes, peeled and thinly sliced
2½ cups jicama, sliced
1½ tablespoons brown sugar

1. In medium saucepan, bring ¾ cup water to a boil. Add carrots and sweet potatoes and simmer until semi-tender. Drain and cool.
2. Heat oven to 350 degrees. Grease a small baking dish.
3. In small baking dish, layer sweet potatoes and carrots with jicama. Sprinkle brown sugar on top.
4. Add ¼ cup water. Cover and bake until jicama is tender, about 20 minutes.
5. Remove cover and bake until lightly browned, about 10 minutes.

Makes 3 cups

½ cup provides ½ cup VEG for a 3-5 year old at snack

Breakfast

Morning Fun Muffin, String Cheese, Peaches, Milk

	Toddler	Pre-School	School Age
Muffin*	1 muffin	1 muffin	2 muffins
String Cheese (1 oz.)	1/2 piece	1/2 piece	1 piece
Peaches	1/4 cup	1/2 cup	1/2 cup
Milk	1/2 cup	3/4 cup	1 cup

Lunch

Chicken Tango Triangles, Spinach Salad, Orange Wedges, Milk

	Toddler	Pre-School	School Age
Sandwiches*	3 triangles	4 triangles	6 triangles
Salad	1/4 cup	1/4 cup	1/2 cup
Oranges	1/8 cup	1/4 cup	1/4 cup
Milk	1/2 cup	3/4 cup	1 cup

Snack

Cheese Crispies, Milk

	Toddler	Pre-School	School Age
Cheese Crispies*	1 crispy	1 crispy	2 crispies
Milk	1/2 cup	1/2 cup	1 cup

WINTER Week 2 Thursday

Breakfast

Morning Fun Muffins

¼ cup butter, softened
2 tablespoons brown sugar, or to taste
1½ cup bananas, mashed
½ cup applesauce
1 cup carrots, grated
1 egg, beaten
½ teaspoon vanilla extract
¾ cup whole wheat flour
½ teaspoon baking soda
½ teaspoon pumpkin pie spice
¼ teaspoon salt

1. Preheat oven to 375 degrees. Grease 6-cup muffin pan or line with paper liners.

2. In a bowl, cream together the butter and brown sugar until fluffy. Mix in the bananas, applesauce, carrots, eggs and vanilla.

3. Stir in the flour, baking soda, pumpkin pie spice and salt until just combined.

4. Spoon batter into the prepared muffin cups.

5. Bake for 15 to 20 minutes. Cool in the pan for 10 minutes before removing to a wire rack.

Makes 6 muffins

  1 muffin provides 0.5 oz. GB
  for a 3-5 year old at breakfast

Lunch

Chicken Tango Triangles

9 ounces cooked chicken, shredded
1 tablespoon mayonnaise
¼ cup green onions, thinly sliced
½ cup tomatoes, diced small
1 cup carrots, grated
6 slices whole grain bread

1. In a medium bowl, mix together the chicken, mayonnaise, onions, tomatoes and carrots.

2. Spread mixture over bread, cut into triangles and serve.

Makes 24 triangles

  4 triangles provide 1 oz. GB,
  1.5 oz. MMA and ¼ cup VEG
  for a 3-5 year old at lunch/supper

Snack

Cheese Crispies

1 cup whole wheat flour
2 teaspoons baking powder
¼ teaspoon paprika
¼ teaspoon salt
2 cups cheddar cheese, grated
1 egg, beaten
¼ cup 1% or fat-free milk
Sesame seeds for garnish

1. In a medium bowl, blend flour, baking powder, paprika and salt.

2. Add grated cheese, egg and milk. Mix all ingredients until dough forms a ball. Cover and refrigerate for 30 minutes.

4. Preheat oven to 350 degrees. Coat baking sheet with non-stick spray.

5. Roll out dough very thin. Cut out circles with cookie cutter or drinking glass and place on baking sheet. Sprinkle with sesame seeds.

6. Bake at 350 degrees until lightly golden and firm, about 15 minutes.

Makes 16 crispies

  1 crispie provides 0.5 oz. MMA
  for a 3-5 year old at snack

WINTER Week 2 Friday

Breakfast

Scrambled Eggs, Whole Grain Cereal, Banana, Milk

	Toddler	Pre-School	School Age
Scrambled Eggs	1/4 cup	1/4 cup	1/2 cup
Cereal Rounds	1/2 cup	1/2 cup	1 cup
Banana	1/2	1	1
Milk	1/2 cup	3/4 cup	1 cup

Lunch

Mighty Meatloaf, Whole Grain Roll, Amazing Acorn Squash, Cantaloupe Bites, Milk

	Toddler	Pre-School	School Age
Meatloaf*	2/3 slice	1 slice	1-1/3 slices
Roll	1/2	1/2	1
Squash*	1 quarter	1 half	2 halves
Cantaloupe	1/8 cup	1/4 cup	1/4 cup
Milk	1/2 cup	3/4 cup	1 cup

Snack

Bunny Juice, Whole Grain Crackers

	Toddler	Pre-School	School Age
Bunny Juice*	1/2 cup	1/2 cup	3/4 cup
Crackers	3	3	6

twist & sprout

164

Lunch

Mighty Meatloaf

1½ tablespoons olive oil
3 tablespoons green bell peppers, chopped
3 tablespoons onions, chopped
2 eggs
½ cup crushed pineapple
3 tablespoons regular rolled oats
1¼ cups breadcrumbs
1½ teaspoons dried Italian seasoning
¾ teaspoon garlic powder
¾ teaspoon salt
¼ teaspoon black pepper
1 pound ground turkey

1. Preheat oven to 350 degrees. Coat loaf pan with non-stick cooking spray.

2. In a skillet, sauté green peppers and onions in the olive oil for 5 minutes. Transfer to a large bowl.

3. Add eggs, pineapple, oats, breadcrumbs and spices to sautéed vegetables and mix well.

4. Add ground turkey to bowl. Mix by hand until well blended.

5. Spoon turkey mixture into loaf pan, packing loosely but evenly.

6. Bake for 75-90 minutes or until internal temperature reaches 165 degrees.

Lunch

7. Remove from oven and cut into 7 slices.

Makes 7 1½-ounce slices

  1 slice provides 1.5 oz. MMA
  for a 3-5 year old at lunch/supper

Amazing Acorn Squash

3 small acorn squash, halved and seeded
3 tablespoons butter
6 tablespoons brown sugar

1. Preheat oven to 400 degrees. Coat baking dish with non-stick spray.

2. Score the inside of each squash half several times with a sharp knife and then place in the baking dish, cut side up. Spread ½ tablespoon of butter and sprinkle 1 tablespoon brown sugar inside each half.

3. Pour about 1 inch of water into the baking dish so the squash doesn't dry out or burn.

4. Bake until the squash is very soft and the tops are browned, 55-65 minutes.

Makes 6 squash halves

  1 squash half provides ¼ cup VEG
  for a 3-5 year old at lunch/supper

Snack

Bunny Juice

¾ cup low-sodium tomato juice
2¼ cups carrots, peeled and chunked
1½ cups cucumbers, chunked

1. Add tomato juice and carrots to blender. Blend until carrots are pureed, about 2-3 minutes.

2. Add cucumbers and blend mixture until smooth.

Makes 3 cups

  ½ cup provides ½ cup VEG for a 3-5 year old
  at snack

WINTER Week 3 Monday

Breakfast

Fruity Toast, Milk

	Toddler	Pre-School	School Age
Fruity Toast*	1/2 slice	1 slice	1 slice
Milk	1/2 cup	3/4 cup	1 cup

Lunch

Beany Pizza Patties, Whole Grain Bun, Spinach Salad, Apple Slices, Milk

	Toddler	Pre-School	School Age
Pizza Patties*	1 patty	1 patty	1-1/2 patties
Bun	1/2	1/2	1
Spinach Salad	1/4 cup	1/2 cup	1 cup
Apple Slices	1/8 cup	1/4 cup	1/4 cup
Milk	1/2 cup	3/4 cup	1 cup

Snack

Turkey Roll-Ups

	Toddler	Pre-School	School Age
Roll-Ups*	4 roll-ups	4 roll-ups	6 roll-ups

Breakfast

Fruity Toast

6 slices whole wheat bread
6 tablespoons low-fat whipped cream cheese
3 cups fruit, sliced, such as banana,
    strawberries, peaches, kiwi

1. Toast bread.

2. Spread each slice with 1 tablespoon cream cheese. Top with ½ cup fresh fruit.

Makes 6 slices

  1 slice provides 1 oz. GB and ½ cup FR
  for a 3-5 year old at breakfast

Lunch

Beany Pizza Patties

1½ cup low-sodium marinara sauce
2 15-ounce cans (3 cups) red kidney beans,
    rinsed and drained
1 egg, beaten
⅓ cup breadcrumbs
1 tablespoon Italian seasoning
¼ teaspoon salt

1. In a saucepan, warm marinara sauce over low heat.

2. In a large bowl, mash the beans. Add the egg, breadcrumbs and spices and combine well. Form 6 patties.

3. Coat a large skillet with non-stick cooking spray and place over medium heat. Add patties and cook until brown and crusty. Flip patties and brown the other side.

4. To serve, pour ¼ cup warm marinara sauce over each patty.

Makes 6 patties

  1 patty with ¼ cup sauce provides 1.5 oz.
  MMA and ¼ cup VEG for a 3-5 year old at
  lunch/supper

Snack

Turkey Roll-Ups

6 ounces low-sodium deli turkey, sliced
6 tablespoons low-fat whipped cream cheese
3 cups cucumber spears

1. Divide turkey slices into 6 1-ounce portions. Spread cream cheese on each portion.

2. Place cucumber spears on the turkey slices and roll up.

3. Cut each turkey roll-up into 4 pieces.

Makes 24 roll-ups

  4 roll-ups provide 1 oz. MMA and
  ½ cup VEG for a 3-5 year old at snack

Breakfast

Berry Blueberry Muffins, Blueberries, Milk

	Toddler	Pre-School	School Age
Muffin*	1/2 muffin	1/2 muffin	1 muffin
Blueberries	1/4 cup	1/2 cup	1/2 cup
Milk	1/2 cup	3/4 cup	1 cup

Lunch

Chicken Bites, Whole Wheat Roll, Tangy Sweet Potatoes, Groovy Grapes, Milk

	Toddler	Pre-School	School Age
Chicken Bites*	4 bites	5 bites	7 bites
Roll	1/2 roll	1/2 roll	1 roll
Sweet Potatoes*	1/8 cup	1/4 cup	1/2 cup
Grapes	1/8 cup	1/4 cup	1/4 cup
Milk	1/2 cup	3/4 cup	1 cup

Snack

Tomato Bruschetta

	Toddler	Pre-School	School Age
Bruschetta*	3 slices	3 slices	5 slices

twist & sprout

Breakfast

Berry Blueberry Muffins

¼ cup regular rolled oats
½ cup 1% or fat-free milk
⅔ cup whole wheat flour
1½ teaspoons baking powder
¼ teaspoon ground cinnamon
⅛ teaspoon salt
3 tablespoons brown sugar
1½ tablespoons vegetable oil
1 teaspoon grated lemon zest
1 egg, lightly beaten
½ cup fresh or frozen blueberries, drained.

1. Preheat oven to 400 degrees. Grease a 6-cup muffin pan or use greased foil cups.

2. In a bowl, combine the oats and milk and microwave on high for 3 minutes.

3. In another bowl, whisk to blend all dry ingredients. Stir in the brown sugar, oil, lemon zest, hot oatmeal and the egg. Gently fold in the blueberries.

4. Spoon batter into muffin cups. Bake 15-18 minutes.

Makes 6 muffins

½ muffin provides 0.5 oz. GB
for a 3-5 year old at breakfast

Lunch

Homemade Chicken Bites

3 eggs, beaten
¾ cup breadcrumbs
¼ teaspoon pepper
¼ teaspoon paprika
½ teaspoon dried parsley
5 tablespoons Parmesan cheese
1 pound boneless, skinless chicken

1. Preheat oven to 400 degrees. Coat baking sheet with non-stick cooking spray or line with lightly-greased foil.

2. In a small bowl, beat the eggs.

3. In a plastic bag, mix the breadcrumbs, pepper, paprika, dried parsley and cheese.

4. Cut the chicken breast into 30 bite-sized chunks.

5. Dip chicken into the beaten eggs and then dredge in the bag of breadcrumbs. Shake to coat all sides and place on baking sheet.

6. Bake for 15-20 minutes.

Makes 30 chicken bites

5 chicken bites provide 1.5 oz. MMA
for a 3-5 year old at lunch/supper

Snack

Easy Tomato Bruschetta

½ of a 12-ounce loaf French bread
  or baguette, cut into 18 slices
3 tablespoons olive oil
3 cups fresh tomatoes, finely diced
¼ cup fresh basil, chopped
⅛ teaspoon salt
⅛ teaspoon pepper

1. Preheat oven to 350 degrees.

2. Place bread slices on baking sheet. Brush tops with olive oil.

3. Bake until toasted, about 5 to 7 minutes.

4. While bread is toasting, combine tomatoes, basil, salt and pepper.

5. Spoon 3 tablespoons of the tomato mixture on each slice of toast.

Makes 18 slices

3 slices provide 1 oz. GB and ½ cup VEG for
a 3-5 year old at snack

Recipe for Tangy Sweet Potatoes
is found on page 186.

Breakfast

Broccoli Mini-Bakes, Whole Grain Toast, Clementines, Milk

	Toddler	Pre-School	School Age
Mini-Bakes*	1/2 mini-bake	1/2 mini-bake	1 mini-bake
Toast	1/2 slice	1/2 slice	1 slice
Clementine	1	2	2
Milk	1/2 cup	3/4 cup	1 cup

Lunch

Potato Vegetable Chowder, Cracker Stackers, Banana, Milk

	Toddler	Pre-School	School Age
Chowder*	1/2 cup	1/2 cup	1 cup
Cracker Stackers*	1	2	2
Banana	1/4	1/2	1/2
Milk	1/2 cup	3/4 cup	1 cup

Snack

Whole Wheat Baking Powder Biscuits, Pears

	Toddler	Pre-School	School Age
Biscuits*	1/2 biscuit	1/2 biscuit	1 biscuit
Pears	1/2 cup	1/2 cup	3/4 cup

Breakfast

Broccoli Mini Bakes

2¼ teaspoons unsalted butter
1½ cups broccoli, chopped
1 cup tomatoes, chopped
½ cup onions, finely chopped
⅛ teaspoon ground cumin
5 eggs
1 cup hash brown potatoes
⅓ cup cheddar cheese, shredded
Salt and pepper, to taste

1. Preheat oven to 400 degrees. Line a 6-cup muffin pan with greased foil cups.

2. In large skillet, heat butter over medium heat. Add broccoli, tomatoes, onions and cumin. Sauté for 5 minutes, or until tender and water evaporates.

3. In large bowl, lightly beat eggs. Add the cooked vegetables, potatoes and cheese. Season with salt and pepper and mix well.

4. Spoon mixture into each muffin cup and bake for 10-20 minutes.

Makes 6 mini bakes

 1 mini bake provides 1 oz. MMA and
 ¼ cup VEG for a 3-5 year old at breakfast

Lunch

Potato Vegetable Chowder

1 tablespoon olive oil
½ cup carrots, peeled and finely chopped
¾ cup onions, finely chopped
¾ cup zucchini, finely chopped
¾ cup leeks, chopped
2 tablespoons fresh garlic, minced
½ teaspoon dried thyme
2½ cups low-sodium vegetable broth
¾ cup diced tomatoes
1 cup unpeeled red potatoes, diced
1 teaspoon salt

1. In a large soup pot, warm the olive oil and sauté the carrots, onions, zucchini, leeks, garlic and thyme for 10 minutes.

2. Add broth, tomatoes, potatoes and salt. Bring to a boil.

3. Reduce heat and simmer until vegetables are completely tender, about 15 minutes.

Makes 6 cups

 ½ cup chowder provides ¼ cup VEG
 for a 3-5 year old at lunch/supper

*Recipe for Cracker Stackers
is found on page 186.*

Snack

Whole Grain Baking Powder Biscuits

¾ cup whole wheat flour
1½ teaspoons baking powder
⅛ teaspoon salt
1½ tablespoons cold butter
⅓ cup 1% or fat-free milk

1. Preheat oven to 450 degrees.

2. In a bowl, combine flour, baking powder and salt.

3. Cut butter into flour mixture until it resembles coarse crumbs. Pour in the milk and mix together.

4. Pat out dough to a ¾-inch thickness. Cut biscuits rounds with a biscuit cutter or the lip of a drinking glass. Place on a baking sheet.

5. Bake until lightly golden, about 10 to 12 minutes.

Makes 6 biscuits

 ½ biscuit provides 0.5 oz. GB
 for a 3-5 year old at lunch/supper

WINTER Week 3 Thursday

Breakfast

Apple Pancakes, Hard Boiled Egg, Milk

	Toddler	Pre-School	School Age
Apple Pancake*	1/2 pancake	1 pancake	1 pancake
Egg	1/2	1/2	1
Milk	1/2 cup	3/4 cup	1 cup

Lunch

Loveable Lentils, Whole Grain Roll, Broccoli Crowns, Pineapple Triangles, Milk

	Toddler	Pre-School	School Age
Lentils*	1/3 cup	1/2 cup	2/3 cup
Roll	1/2	1/2	1
Broccoli	1/8 cup	1/4 cup	1/2 cup
Pineapple	1/8 cup	1/4 cup	1/4 cup
Milk	1/2 cup	3/4 cup	1 cup

Snack

Tomato Treats

	Toddler	Pre-School	School Age
Tomato Treats*	2 treats	2 treats	4 treats

Breakfast

Apple Pancakes

¾ cup whole wheat flour
¾ teaspoon baking powder
⅛ teaspoon salt
1 egg
⅓ cup 1% or fat-free milk
1½ cups green apples, cored and grated
2¼ cups fresh fruit, chopped

1. In a bowl, combine flour, baking powder, salt.

2. In a separate bowl, whisk together the egg and milk. Stir in the grated apples until just incorporated.

3. Add apple-egg mixture to the dry ingredients, stirring gently.

4. Coat large skillet with non-stick cooking spray and heat over medium heat.

5. Pour ⅓ cup batter for each pancake into skillet. Cook until crisp and then flip to cook the other side.

6. To serve, top each pancake with ⅓ cup fruit.

Makes 6 pancakes

1 pancake with ⅓ cup fruit topping provides 1 oz. GB and ½ cup FR for a 3-5 year old at breakfast

Lunch

Lovable Lentils

1 cup water
⅔ cup dry lentils, rinsed
⅓ cup onions, chopped
1 medium carrot, thinly sliced
¼ cup celery, thinly sliced
1 clove fresh garlic, minced
½ teaspoon salt
⅛ teaspoon pepper
⅛ teaspoon **EACH** of dried marjoram, sage, thyme
1 bay leaf
¾ cup fresh or canned tomatoes, diced
¼ cup green bell peppers, chopped
2 teaspoons fresh parsley, minced
1 cup (4 ounces) cheese, shredded

1. Preheat oven to 350 degrees. Coat a 9 x 13-inch baking dish with non-stick cooking spray.

2. In the baking dish, stir together the first 10 ingredients (water through bay leaf).

3. Cover and bake for 45 minutes.

4. Stir in tomatoes and green peppers. Cover and bake an additional 15 minutes.

5. Sprinkle with parsley and cheese. Bake, uncovered, for 5-10 minutes or until cheese is melted. Discard bay leaf before serving.

Makes 3½ cups

½ cup provides 1.5 oz. MMA for a 3-5 year old at lunch/supper

Snack

Tomato Treats

3 cups tomatoes, sliced (12 slices total)
1½ cups cottage cheese
¼ cup balsamic vinegar

1. Arrange tomato slices on a plate. Top each slice with 2 tablespoons of cottage cheese and then drizzle with 1 teaspoon vinegar.

Makes 12 tomato treats

2 tomato treats provides 0.5 oz. MMA and ½ cup VEG for a 3-5 year old at snack

Breakfast

Whole Grain English Muffin, Nut Butter, Curried Peachy Pears, Milk

	Toddler	Pre-School	School Age
Muffin	1/2 muffin	1/2 muffin	1 muffin
Nut Butter	1 tbsp	1 tbsp	2 tbsp
Pears*	1/4 cup	1/2 cup	1/2 cup
Milk	1/2 cup	3/4 cup	1 cup

Lunch

Teriyaki Chicken, Savory Brown Rice, Carrot Sticks, Green Pepper Strips, Milk

	Toddler	Pre-School	School Age
Chicken*	1 drumstick	1 drumstick	2 drumsticks
Brown Rice*	1/4 cup	1/4 cup	1/2 cup
Carrot Sticks	1/8 cup	1/4 cup	1/2 cup
Green Peppers	1/8 cup	1/4 cup	1/4 cup
Milk	1/2 cup	3/4 cup	1 cup

Snack

Cranberry-Apple Salad, Milk

	Toddler	Pre-School	School Age
Cranberry Salad*	1/2 cup	1/2 cup	3/4 cup
Milk	1/2 cup	1/2 cup	1 cup

twist & sprout

Breakfast

Curried Peachy Pears

1 tablespoon butter
1 teaspoon curry powder
2 15-ounce cans sliced peaches, drained
1 15-ounce can sliced pears, drained
1 tablespoon brown sugar

1. Melt butter in sauté pan over medium heat.

2. Add curry powder, fruit and brown sugar. Mix well. Cook until fruit is heated through.

Makes 3 cups

½ cup provides ½ cup FR
for a 3-5 year old at breakfast

Snack

Cranberry-Apple Salad

¾ cup fresh cranberries, chopped
¾ cup red apples, chopped
1½ cups seedless green grapes, chopped
¼ cup raisins
6 ounces vanilla low-fat yogurt

1. In a bowl, toss all ingredients with the yogurt. Cover and chill for 2 hours. Stir before serving.

Makes 3 cups

½ cup provides ½ cup FR
for a 3-5 year old at snack

Lunch

Teriyaki Chicken

2 tablespoons lemon juice
1½ tablespoons low-sodium soy sauce
1½ tablespoons vegetable oil
2 teaspoons ketchup
⅛ teaspoon black pepper
⅛ teaspoon garlic powder
6 skinless chicken drumsticks

1. Lightly oil a shallow baking pan.

2. In a bowl, stir together until smooth the lemon juice, soy sauce, vegetable oil, ketchup, pepper and garlic powder.

3. Lay the chicken in the baking pan and pour the marinade over them. Cover and refrigerate overnight.

4. Preheat oven to 350 degrees.

5. Bake until the internal temperature of the chicken has reached 165 degrees, about 45 minutes.

Makes 6 drumsticks

1 drumstick provides 1.5 oz. MMA
for a 3-5 year old at lunch/supper

Lunch

Savory Brown Rice

¾ cup brown rice
1½ cups water
⅛ teaspoon salt

1. Add the rice, water and salt to a saucepan.

2. Cover and bring to a boil. Without removing the lid, immediately reduce heat to the lowest setting and cook 30 minutes.

3. Remove lid and fluff the rice. Test for doneness. Add a little water, cover and continue to cook until rice is soft, about 10-15 more minutes.

Makes 1½ cups

¼ cup rice provides 0.5 oz. GB
for a 3-5 year old at lunch/supper

WINTER Week 4 Monday

Breakfast

Sunshine Scrambler, Whole Grain Toast, Mandarin Oranges, Milk

	Toddler	Pre-School	School Age
Scrambler*	1/4 cup	1/2 cup	1/2 cup
Toast	1/2 slice	1/2 slice	1 slice
Mandarin Oranges	1/4 cup	1/2 cup	1/2 cup
Milk	1/2 cup	3/4 cup	1 cup

Lunch

Tasty Tomato-Basil Pasta, Cucumber Wheels, Banana, Milk

	Toddler	Pre-School	School Age
Pasta*	1/2 cup	3/4 cup	1 cup
Cucumbers	1/8 cup	1/4 cup	1/2 cup
Banana	1/4	1/2	1/2
Milk	1/2 cup	3/4 cup	1 cup

Snack

Apple-Rice Delight

	Toddler	Pre-School	School Age
Apple-Rice Delight*	3/4 cup	3/4 cup	1-1/2 cup

176

Breakfast

Sunshine Scrambler

2 tablespoons olive oil
½ cup red or green bell peppers, chopped
½ cup tomatoes, chopped
6 eggs, beaten
¼ cup Parmesan cheese, shredded

1. In a medium sauté pan, heat oil over medium heat. Add bell peppers and tomatoes and sauté until peppers are tender, about 2 minutes.

2. Add eggs. Stir and cook until firm, solid and not clear, about 2-3 minutes.

3. Portion, garnish with shredded cheese and serve.

Makes 3 cups

½ cup provides 1 oz. MMA
for a 3-5 year old at breakfast

Lunch

Tasty Tomato-Basil Pasta

1½ teaspoons olive oil
8 ounces lean ground turkey
2 teaspoons fresh garlic, minced
2 teaspoons dried leaf basil
¾ teaspoon Italian seasoning
3 cups cooked whole wheat rotini or penne pasta
11 ounces canned crushed tomatoes
¾ cup cottage cheese
¼ cup Parmesan cheese
¾ cup mozzarella cheese

1. Preheat oven to 350 degrees. Coat a 9 x 13-inch baking dish with non-stick cooking spray.

2. Heat oil in a skillet. Add ground turkey and spices and cook until done.

3. In large bowl, combine tomatoes, cottage cheese, cooked turkey mixture and Parmesan cheese. Mix well. Add cooked pasta.

4. Pour the pasta mixture into the baking dish and sprinkle with the mozzarella cheese.

5. Bake for 30 minutes.

Makes 6 cups

¾ cup provides 0.5 oz. GB and 1.5 oz. MMA
for a 3-5 year old at lunch/supper

Snack

Apple-Rice Delight

1½ cups cooked rice
1½ cups applesauce
1½ teaspoons ground cinnamon
1½ cups vanilla low-fat yogurt

1. In a large bowl, mix rice and applesauce together in a large bowl.

2. Add cinnamon and yogurt. Stir well.

Makes 4½ cups

¾ cup provides 0.5 oz. GB and 0.5 oz. MMA
for a 3-5 year old at snack

Breakfast

Mexican Migas, Banana, Milk

	Toddler	Pre-School	School Age
Egg Migas*	1/2 portion	1/2 portion	1 portion
Banana	1/2	1	1
Milk	1/2 cup	3/4 cup	1 cup

Lunch

Wonderful Winter Soup, Whole Wheat Roll, Peaches, Milk

	Toddler	Pre-School	School Age
Soup*	2/3 cup	1 cup	1-1/3 cups
Roll	1/2 roll	1/2 roll	1 roll
Peaches	1/8 cup	1/4 cup	1/4 cup
Milk	1/2 cup	3/4 cup	1 cup

Snack

Blizzard Fruit Mix, Milk

	Toddler	Pre-School	School Age
Fruit Mix*	1/2 cup	1/2 cup	3/4 cup
Milk	1/2 cup	1/2 cup	1 cup

twist & sprout

Breakfast

Mexican Migas

2 tablespoons butter
6 8-inch corn tortillas,
   cut into long, narrow strips
½ teaspoon salt
¼ teaspoon black pepper
6 large eggs, beaten
½ cup cheese, shredded
1 cup salsa

1. In a large pan, melt the butter. Add the tortilla strips and cook, stirring occasionally, until they start to get slightly golden. Season with salt and pepper.

2. Pour the eggs into the pan over the tortilla strips and cook, stirring occasionally, until the eggs are almost fully cooked but still a little wet.

3. Stir in the cheese and finish cooking the eggs.

4. To serve, divide into 6 portions and top each with 2 tablespoons salsa.

Makes 6 portions

  1 portion provides 1 oz. GB and 2 oz. MMA
  for a 3-5 year old at breakfast

Lunch

Wonderful Winter Soup

2 tablespoons olive oil
½ cup onions, chopped
½ cup carrots, peeled and chopped
½ cup celery, chopped
2 cups (1 lb.) butternut squash,
   peeled and cubed
1 teaspoon dried leaf thyme
1 tablespoon fresh garlic, minced
1½ teaspoons dried leaf parsley
2 cups low-sodium vegetable stock
⅓ cup bulgur wheat
2 15-ounce cans (3 cups) chickpeas,
   rinsed and drained
½ cup canned petite diced tomatoes

1. In a large stock pot, heat oil and sauté onions, carrots and celery for 5 minutes.

2. Add squash, thyme, garlic and parsley. Add vegetable stock and bring to a simmer. Cook until squash is tender, about 10 to 15 minutes.

3. Add bulgur, chickpeas and tomatoes. Simmer another 10 minutes.

Makes 6 cups

  1 cup provides 1.5 oz. MMA and ½ cup VEG
  for a 3-5 year old at lunch/supper

Snack

Blizzard Fruit Mix

1½ cups apples, cored, chopped
¾ cup red or green grapes, halved
1 14½-ounce can peaches,
   drained and chopped

1. Mix apples, grapes and peaches together.

Makes 3 cups

  ½ cup provides ½ cup FR
  for a 3-5 year old at snack

Breakfast

Goldilocks Porridge, Blueberries, Milk

	Toddler	Pre-School	School Age
Porridge*	1/4 cup	1/4 cup	1/2 cup
Blueberries	1/4 cup	1/2 cup	1/2 cup
Milk	1/2 cup	3/4 cup	1 cup

Lunch

Pizza Wheels, Broccoli Trees, Apple Wedges, Milk

	Toddler	Pre-School	School Age
Pizza Wheels*	1/2 wheel	1 wheel	1 wheel
Broccoli	1/8 cup	1/4 cup	1/2 cup
Apple Wedges	1/8 cup	1/4 cup	1/4 cup
Milk	1/2 cup	3/4 cup	1 cup

Snack

Crispy Carrot Coleslaw, Milk

	Toddler	Pre-School	School Age
Coleslaw*	2/3 cup	2/3 cup	1 cup
Milk	1/2 cup	1/2 cup	1 cup

Breakfast

Goldilocks Porridge

4 cups 1% or fat-free milk
1 cinnamon stick
¼ teaspoon salt
¾ cup whole grain farina

1. In a saucepan, bring milk, cinnamon stick and salt just to a boil.

2. Gradually add farina, stirring constantly with wire whisk until well blended.

3. Return to a boil. Reduce heat to low and simmer uncovered, stirring frequently, until thickened, about 8 minutes.

4. Remove cinnamon stick before serving.

Makes 1½ cups

 ¼ cup provides 0.5 oz. GB
 for a 3-5 year old at breakfast

Lunch

Pizza Wheels

1 cup whole wheat flour
⅛ teaspoon salt
1¾ teaspoons active dry yeast
⅓ cup 1% or fat-free milk, warmed
2 teaspoons olive oil
¼ cup tomato sauce
¾ teaspoon Italian seasoning
⅓ cup onions, finely chopped
⅓ cup green bell peppers, finely chopped
8 ounces ham, finely chopped
2 cups mozzarella cheese, grated

1. Preheat oven to 350 degrees. Coat a baking sheet with non-stick cooking spray.

2. In a bowl, combine flour, salt and yeast. Add warm milk and oil and mix. Knead 5 minutes.

3. Roll out to make a 12 x 8-inch rectangle.

4. Spread tomato sauce over dough and sprinkle with the Italian seasoning, onions, peppers, ham and cheese. Roll up lengthwise, jelly roll-style. Cut into 8 slices and lay them on baking sheet.

5. Bake for 25 minutes.

Makes 8 pizza wheels

 1 wheel provides 1 oz. GB and 2 oz. MMA
 for a 3-5 year old at lunch/supper

Snack

Crispy Carrot Coleslaw

1½ cups (green, red or both) cabbage, shredded
1½ cups carrots, peeled and shredded
½ cup raisins
¼ cup apples, cored and chopped small
¼ cup crushed pineapple, drained
¼ cup light mayonnaise

1. In a large bowl, mix the cabbage, carrots, raisins, apples and pineapple with the mayonnaise.

2. Cover and refrigerate a minimum of one hour before serving.

Makes about 4 cups

 ⅔ cup provides ½ cup VEG
 for a 3-5 year old at snack

WINTER Week 4 Thursday

Breakfast

Cranberry-Sweet Potato Muffins, Pineapple Triangles, Milk

	Toddler	Pre-School	School Age
Muffin*	1/2 muffin	1/2 muffin	1 muffin
Pineapple	1/4 cup	1/2 cup	1/2 cup
Milk	1/2 cup	3/4 cup	1 cup

Lunch

Chicken Caesar Wraps, Carrot Spears, Great Grapes, Milk

	Toddler	Pre-School	School Age
Wraps*	1/2 wrap	1 wrap	1 wrap
Carrot Spears	1/8 cup	1/8 cup	1/4 cup
Grapes	1/8 cup	1/4 cup	1/4 cup
Milk	1/2 cup	3/4 cup	1 cup

Snack

Rosy Mozzarella Bites, Milk

	Toddler	Pre-School	School Age
Mozzarella Bites*	2 bites	3 bites	3 bites
Milk	1/2 cup	1/2 cup	1 cup

182

Breakfast

Cranberry Sweet-Potato Muffins

Muffins
¾ cup whole wheat flour
3 tablespoons sugar
1 teaspoon baking powder
¼ teaspoon salt
¼ teaspoon ground cinnamon
¼ cup cooked sweet potatoes, mashed
2 tablespoons 1% or fat-free milk
2 tablespoons melted butter
1 egg
½ cup fresh or frozen cranberries, chopped

Topping
1 tablespoon sugar
½ teaspoon ground cinnamon

1. Preheat oven to 375 degrees. Grease a 6-cup muffin pan or line with paper liners.

2. In a large bowl, whisk together flour, sugar, baking powder, salt, cinnamon.

3. In a separate bowl, stir together the sweet potatoes, milk, butter and egg.

4. Add the wet ingredients to the dry ingredients. Stir until just combined. Fold in cranberries. Spoon batter into muffin cups.

Lunch

5. Make topping by mixing together the sugar and cinnamon. Sprinkle over batter.

6. Bake for 18-22 minutes.

Makes 6 muffins

> 1 muffin provides 0.5 oz. GB
> for a 3-5 year old at breakfast

Lunch

Chicken Caesar Wraps

6 cups romaine lettuce, shredded
¼ cup Caesar dressing
3 12-inch whole wheat tortillas
12 ounces cooked chicken, shredded

1. In a bowl, toss the lettuce with the Caesar dressing.

2. Top each tortilla with 4 ounces chicken and 2 cups lettuce.

3. Roll tightly and cut in half.

Makes 6 wraps

> 1 wrap provides 1 oz. GB, 2 oz. MMA and
> ½ cup VEG for a 3-5 year old at lunch/supper

Snack

Rosy Mozzarella Bites

18 large whole grain crackers
1½ cups mozzarella cheese, shredded
¾ cup spaghetti sauce, at room temperature

1. Preheat oven to 350 degrees. Coat baking sheet with non-stick cooking spray.

2. Place crackers on baking sheet pan and sprinkle with cheese.

3. Bake until cheese begins to melt, about 5 minutes.

4. Remove crackers from oven and top with 2 teaspoons of spaghetti sauce.

Makes 18 bites

> 3 bites provide 1 oz. GB and 1 oz. MMA
> for a 3-5 year old at snack

WINTER Week 4 Friday

Breakfast

Zesty Breakfast Wrap, Milk

	Toddler	Pre-School	School Age
Zesty Wrap*	1 wrap	2 wraps	2 wraps
Milk	1/2 cup	3/4 cup	1 cup

Lunch

Oven Beef Stew, Whole Grain Crackers, Orange Smiles, Milk

	Toddler	Pre-School	School Age
Beef Stew*	2/3 cup	1 cup	1-1/3 cups
Crackers	3	3	6
Orange Smiles	1/8 cup	1/4 cup	1/4 cup
Milk	1/2 cup	3/4 cup	1 cup

Snack

Spinach Boats

	Toddler	Pre-School	School Age
Spinach Boats*	1 boat	1 boat	1-1/2 boats

twist & sprout

Breakfast

Zesty Breakfast Wraps

1 15-ounce can (1½ cups) pinto beans, rinsed and drained
1 14½-ounce can diced tomatoes
½ cup yellow onions, finely chopped
1 teaspoon fresh garlic, minced
¼ cup salsa
¾ cup cheddar cheese, shredded
6 8-inch whole wheat tortillas

1. In a large saucepan over medium heat, bring the beans, tomatoes, onions, garlic and salsa to a simmer. Cook until onions are tender, about 10 minutes.

2. Remove from heat, add cheese and mix well.

3. To assemble, spread about ⅔ cup of the bean mixture on each tortilla. Roll up tortillas and cut in half.

Makes 12 wraps

2 wraps provide 1 oz. GB and ½ cup VEG for a 3-5 year old at breakfast

Lunch

Oven Beef Stew

1 pound beef chuck, cut into pieces
¼ cup flour
¾ teaspoon salt
½ teaspoon pepper
½ teaspoon paprika
2 teaspoons Italian seasoning
½ cup onions, chopped
1 cup carrots, peeled and chunked
1 cup potatoes, peeled and chunked
1 cup low-sodium chicken broth
1 14½-ounce can diced tomatoes

1. Preheat oven to 400 degrees. Spray a baking dish with non-stick cooking spray.

2. In a large bowl, combine flour and spices. Add stew meat and toss well to coat all pieces. Place meat in the baking dish and bake, uncovered, for 30 minutes.

3. Add onions, carrots, potatoes, broth and tomatoes to the baking dish.

4. Reduce heat to 375 degrees. Cover the dish and cook for 2 hours, stirring thoroughly halfway through cooking.

Makes 6 cups

1 cup provides 1.5 oz. MMA and ½ cup VEG for a 3-5 year old at lunch/supper

Snack

Tuna Spinach Boats

1 5-ounce can water-packed tuna, drained
½ cup celery, chopped
2 tablespoons light mayonnaise
1 teaspoon vinegar
6 cups fresh spinach leaves
½ cup sunflower seeds

1. In a bowl, mix together the drained tuna, celery, mayonnaise and vinegar.

2. To serve, make a "boat" of 1 cup spinach leaves on each plate and spoon ¼ cup tuna salad into each one.

3. Top each "boat" with 1 heaping tablespoon of sunflower seeds.

Makes 6 boats

1 boat provides 1 oz. MMA and ½ cup VEG for a 3-5 year old at snack

Recipes

Lunch

Tangy Sweet Potatoes

3 cups sweet potatoes, peeled and diced
¾ cup onions, chopped
3 tablespoons Parmesan cheese
3 tablespoons olive oil

1. Preheat oven to 375 degrees. Line a baking sheet with foil or parchment paper, or coat with non-stick cooking spray.

2. In a large bowl, toss together the sweet potatoes, onions, Parmesan cheese and oil.
3. Spread on baking sheet in a single layer. Roast until tender, about 25-35 minutes.

Makes 3 cups

½ cup provides ½ cup VEG
for a 3-5 year old at lunch/supper

*Tangy Sweet Potatoes are on the
lunch menu for
Winter, Week 3, Tuesday.
See page 168.*

Lunch

Cracker Stackers

36 whole grain crackers
12 ounces low-sodium deli turkey, sliced
¾ cup tomatoes, sliced
¾ cup cucumbers, sliced

1. On each cracker, stack 1 ounce turkey and top with another cracker.

2. Next, stack 1 slice each of the tomato and cucumber, then top with another cracker.

Makes 12 cracker stackers

2 cracker stackers provide 1 oz. GB,
2 oz. MMA and ¼ cup VEG for a 3-5
year old at lunch/supper

*Cracker Stackers are on the lunch menu for
Winter, Week 3, Wednesday.
See page 170.*

Index